POETRY DIMENSION
ANNUAL 3

Edited by DANNIE ABSE

POETRY DIMENSION ANNUAL 3

The Best of the Poetry Year

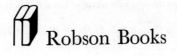 Robson Books

FIRST PUBLISHED IN GREAT BRITAIN IN 1975
BY ROBSON BOOKS LTD., 28 POLAND STREET,
LONDON W1V 3DB. THIS COLLECTION COPY-
RIGHT © DANNIE ABSE 1975

The publishers acknowledge with thanks the assistance of
The Arts Council of Great Britain.

Hardback ISBN 0 903895 51 X
Paperback ISBN 0 903895 52 8

Acknowledgments are owed to the authors whose work has
been reprinted here and which remains their copyright:
also to those publishers and periodicals named below the
prose and poems printed in these pages.

Printed in Great Britain by Hazell Watson & Viney Ltd,
Aylesbury, Bucks

CONTENTS

Introductory note

Criticism

Poems from Books

Points of View

Poems from Magazines

Lives of the Poets

Introductory note

All the poems and most of the prose in this annual have been taken from books and magazines published in Britain since March 1974. Because there are at present a surprising number of genuine poets at work in Britain – young and old, new and established – no difficulty arose in selecting admirable and indeed exciting verse; but serious, readable criticism of contemporary British poetry is harder to come by. There may have been a time when the cry for more poetry and less talk about poetry was just. This is no longer so. The continuing health of contemporary British poetry depends upon an increasing availability of pertinent and extended criticism. The little magazines because of economic reasons are unable to carry essays of any length. All the greater then is the responsibility of more lavish periodicals such as *The New Review* which until now has disappointed so many of us. Fortunately not all is on the debit side. *The Critical Quarterly*, though less lively than in former days, is still thriving as are *The London Magazine* and *Encounter*; and the new *Poetry Nation* is a decided bonus. In any event there is no reason to be defensive about the prose included in these pages and I feel confident that the poems also truly represent the Best of the Poetry Year in Britain now.

D.A.

March 21st 1975

Criticism

Criticism

One of the last times I saw Kathleen Raine, in a late summer visit to London, we talked about the brilliant Cambridge poets of her youth, Empson, Ronald Bottrall, her own former husband, Charles Madge. Miss Raine said to me that she now resented very much being thought of as a poet of that Cambridge school, in so far as there was a school. She now saw that the three figures she mentioned were essentially poets of cleverness, of wit, producing the verse equivalent of prize undergraduate essays, whereas she from the first, however hesitantly at first, had been a poet of vision. If there was any poet who had been at Cambridge with whom she felt a deep affinity, it was Vernon Watkins, a religious visionary like herself. Fond as she was of Empson, and dear friend as he had been, she had avoided seeing him in recent years, because she felt he was a captain in an opposite camp. Yet, with her essential fairness of mind, she added that the first volume of Empson's poems, the 1935 one (she has no liking for *The Gathering Storm*) did express memorably, and with the proper poetic equipment, a universal experience, the agony of youth, the agony, perhaps, simply of being young. Empson had turned, she thought, mainly to criticism in his later years because life had never again offered him such a set of provocations to fine poetry as simply being at once very intelligent (he had remained very intelligent) and at the same time very bewildered and unhappy.

It is in fact Empson's second volume, *The Gathering Storm*, a much more straightforward and a much more outward turned volume, one concerned not with private agony but with the public predicaments of the late 1930s, that has been a great influence on younger poets, from about 1948 onwards, when John Wain published a long pioneer essay on Empson's poetry in John Lehmann's *Penguin New Writing*. The bewildering intricacies and contortions of the 1935 volume were, whether one thought them deplorable or wonderful, inimitable; the villanelles, the poems with refrains subtly shifting their meaning, like 'Aubade', which is not in villanelle form, the poems in *terza rima* with a hanging line at the end, the extreme regularity of metrical form of most of the poems in *The Gathering Storm*, the diction, also, plain, direct, and colloquial without being 'low', lent themselves admirably to imitation. The mode of emotional understatement, a certain blunt and humorous stoicism, a dogged Englishness (nobody could be more English than Empson, even when the setting of his poems is China or Japan) all appealed to what, from the date of their earliest volumes and pamphlets, one can call 'the generation of 1953'. In a strange way, Empson found his first poetic contemporaries among poets, like John Wain, about twenty years younger than himself. I do not know how far he was flattered by such imitations. In a review of an anthology, *Springtime*, edited by Ian Fletcher and myself, Edwin Muir remarked that it was easy enough to imitate some of the surface characteristics of Empson's verse: but that what gave that verse its distinction was not its mannerisms, but its passion.

In at least two other essays, I have dealt in some technical detail with particular poems of Empson's. In a tribute of this sort, it is better to paint with a broad brush, and to try to say what the poems mean to one, after one has lived with them for half a lifetime or so. I think that Empson's immediate contemporaries made, on the whole, very little of them. I remember, in Egypt during the war, that fine neglected poet, Bernard Spencer, telling me that he liked the sound and the gestures of the 1935 volume, but found the sense too intricate and riddling to be worth working out: it was, for all its 'rough magic' or rough music, crossword-puzzle poetry. I said that with the help of Empson's notes I had worked out the sense, but today perhaps I have lost that youthful agility of mind, or eagerness of purpose, that would help me to work it out again.

When I hear Empson read his poems aloud, his earlier poems particularly (I do not find the sense of *most* of the poems in *The Gathering Storm* very difficult) I am reassured, I suppose, by knowing that there *is* a sense, but what captivates me is the mastery of rhythm revealed in Empson's reading, and the absolute confidence of command over the audience revealed in his tone. One of the few contemporary poets for whom Empson has a whole-hearted admiration is Robert Lowell. Lowell's earlier volumes have the same contorted strength as Empson's *Poems* of 1935, and with *Life Studies* he made a transition, rather like the transition in *The Gathering Storm*, to a poetry of sometimes startling informality and deliberate abrupt gaucheness, a poetry, so to say, jettisoning the 'poetic' (though Lowell, of course, does later take up the 'poetic' again, in a publicly eloquent vein). Lowell, on a visit to me at Leicester to give a poetry reading, a visit during which William and Hetta Empson were also my guests, read his audience parts of what is often thought of as his greatest poem of his earlier phase, 'The Quaker Graveyard in Nantuckett'. He explained that, reading this poem over silently to himself, he could still make out what he was intending, when he wrote it, to say; but that reading it aloud, performing it, he had to forget all that, forget the 'deep meanings' and simply ride along with the rhythms. I am sure that Empson still could, though he very sensibly would not, make a prose paraphrase of his earlier poems. But, reading them aloud, as he has done, like Lowell, to a large audience mainly of Leicester students and young people, but on a different occasion, he rides on the rhythms: and he can

15

hold an audience of very young people, the same sort of audience that responds to Brian Patten or Adrian Mitchell, not, certainly, because they are performing the impossible task of doing a practical critical, analytical task while they listen, but because Empson's *broad* semantics in poetry (the planting and repetition of words with a strong emotive charge) enable a listener to stop worrying about the *narrow* semantics, and to be carried on by the authority of tone and the wonderfully effective, usually expressive rather than euphonious rhythms. Empson could make a living on the circuits, if he wanted to. He is the only poet of his generation towards whom I have found, in my students and in young people in my Poetry Workshop evening classes, an unfeigned response.

The whole question that I have been raising, in a rather amateurish way, is really the question of the relationship between what Saussure called *le signifiant* and *le signifié* in poetry. I owe most of the insights in the following two or three pages to conversations with my colleague, Dr Veronica Forrest-Thomson,* who is working on a book on the aesthetics of poetry, or on poetics, in which Empson's earlier poems (which have never been adequately critically examined by anybody, certainly not by myself) will provide one of her main areas of examination. Very roughly speaking, *le signifiant* is, in the context of poetry, such elements as rhythm, metre, alliteration, rhyme, grammar, effects got from the handling in a poem both of the grammatical substructure and the rhythmical superstructure (we write poems, mostly, in correct grammatical sentences and we superimpose upon the sentence structure an equally rigorous line and sometimes stanza structure): *le signifié* is the 'meaning', the extractable sense, the content or range of reference of the poem, in so far as we could ever get at that while jettisoning the verbal handling. Words of course

16

refer, poems in the end make some sort of sense, but we are attracted to a poem by *le signifiant*, we can recognize whether it is grammatically correct and rhythmically attractive, whether it 'works' as a poem, long before we are able to attempt to isolate *le signifié*, the paraphrasable prose content, the 'meaning'.

After all, the 'meaning' in poems is often a very odd sort of meaning. Wordsworth *knows* that the cuckoo is a bird and not a wandering voice, Keats knows that nightingales have a very small average life-span as compared to man, Shelley knows that the skylark is not a blithe spirit and not singing to express any emotions comparable to human emotions in any way; and all three poets know that the birds are not listening to them, and cannot be expected to answer back. Conventions like this, which would seem crazy in life, are part of the tradition as a high-level artifice, or a complex convention imposed upon and questionably juxtaposing other conventions, equally rigid but of a simpler kind:

> *O cuckoo, shall I call thee bird*
> *Or but a wandering voice?*
> *State the alternative preferred*
> *With reasons for your choice.*

This is peculiarly effective, Dr Forrest-Thomson points out, because two equally rigid conventions – the afflatus of the ode, the dry rigour of the examination question – are imposed on each other, making us question each, and yet the result is perfectly adequate in the *signifiant*, in rhyme, rhythm, and correct grammatical structure.

Her example of something very dull and not worth doing in poetry would be the flat imitation in verse of a statement which would be dull and ordinary, and indeed hardly worth making in ordinary life: Kingsley Amis's,

*Shaving this morning, I looked out of the
window . . .*

I pointed out to Dr Forrest-Thomson, however, in
the seminar where this came up, that a reader who
took 'this morning' not as an adverbial qualification
of the participle 'shaving' but as its direct object,
the line would become a very interesting line by her
standards. The thought of Kingsley Amis under-
taking the awesome and indeed almost unimaginable
task of shaving the morning, and yet remaining non-
chalant enough to look out of the window at the
same time is a poetic thought. Old discussions by
myself, Alvarez, F. W. Bateson, of the difficulties,
say, of 'The Teasers and the Dreams' back in the
early 1950s seem by comparison to belong to the
horse-and-buggy age, and I can understand why to-
day bright young Oxford people no longer belong to
the Critical Society or attend, say, Roy Fuller's lec-
tures much. They might be attracted by somebody
like Dr Forrest-Thomson who wants to insist both
that poetry ought to draw attention to its own arbit-
rariness and artifice, and yet seem necessary too:
just as it is arbitrary that 'cat' means cat – the word
in sound or printed shape has no resemblance to the
creature – but necessary, and rational, that 'cat'
means cat, *if you are talking the English language.*
Her sense that in a poem as a small system, just as
in language as a large system, every element is and
should be seen as arbitrary but that the *whole* is
rational and necessary, ought to throw a dazzling
light on the early poems. Our old way of saying, 'It
sounds all right but I can't get the hang of it', was
by comparison very amateurish and clumsy.

There might, of course, be less flattering explana-
tions. Empson's poems might continue to entrance a
new generation, which has almost nothing in com-
mon, for instance, with the generation that first fell
for them, John Wain's, in a big way, because *no*

definite message can be got out of them. Reviewing a volume of essays of mine, *Vision and Rhetoric*, in Eirene Skilbeck's *Twentieth Century*, Donald Davie said that my best essay was that on Empson, because Empson was essentially a poet of tone (in I. A. Richards's sense, a tactful handling of the imagined reader's social responses), and that I was good at talking about tone, but not so good at grasping grand intellectual structures. Empson, Davie seemed to imply, gave in poetry a wonderful impression of a man talking intelligently, but you could not carry away in the end any coherent account of what he had said. At a Critical Society meeting in Oxford in the early 1950s, Alvarez, then a research student working on the school of Donne, may have had a similar point in mind when he described Empson as essentially a 'grammatical' poet. Like many remarks which one fails utterly to understand, this struck me as probably very profound, if one had understood it. (The remark has been puzzling me for twenty years or more but at the moment of writing this it occurs to me that Alvarez may have had the medieval trivium in mind and have been asserting that Empson is a *grammatical* rather than a *rhetorical* or a *logical* poet – let alone, if we bring in the quad-rivium, a *musical* poet. If we translate these medieval terms into modern language, Alvarez may have been meaning that Empson's great gift is to exploit the concessive-aggressive hesitancies and stutters of English syntax – like 'Not but . . .', like, in his prose writing and conversation, 'To be sure . . .' ('I admit that, it's obvious, but it's irrelevant to what we're talking about, though I can see your sly reasons for bringing it up!') or 'Of course . . .' ('I am asserting that everybody accepts this because I know they don't. I am banging down a ten or a jack on the table with the assurance that will make everybody agree it is an ace'). Grammar is partly a game; Empson loves games, and I remember a pleasant morning in a Hampstead pub when he was trying to teach me, abortively I am afraid, to play shove ha'penny.

One is getting far away from the poems, but not so very far away, for the poems are also the person. Briefly I would say that I think Empson is a very splendid poet indeed, and that the ideas, though put forward by such distinguished characters as Alvarez and Davie, that he uses poetry merely as a grammatical trampoline or a tonal sounding board are nonsense. I think there are some bad poems, for instance his long *tour de force* poem, 'Bacchus', is a succession of ingenious Clevelandisms: it is so sharp, it cuts itself. But the early poems do seem to me to express not only the agony, as Kathleen Raine calls it, but the splendour of youth. Anyone who has read them once can never fail to eternally remember these two great stanzas, in an adaptation of Marvell's 'Horatian Ode' metre, from 'This Last Pain', from the 1935 volume:

> *All these large dreams by which men long live well*
> *Are magic-lanterned on the smoke of hell;*
> *This then is real, I have implied,*
> *A painted, small transparent slide.*

> *These the inventive can hand-paint at leisure*
> *Or most emporia would stock our measure*
> *And, feasting in their dappled shade*
> *We should forget how they were made*

And there is the other great stanza, which I quote from memory, but I trust not incorrectly:

> *Imagine, then, by miracle, with me,*
> *(Ambiguous gifts, as what gods give must be)*
> *What could not possibly be there,*
> *And learn a style from a despair.*

This poem was a response to the view of I. A. Richards, Empson's mentor in his later years at

Cambridge, that the outer universe is neutral, it neither hates nor loves nor has any real interest in us, and that when the poet says all's well with the world he cannot mean more, in the cash value of his meaning – whatever he *intends* to mean – than that all is well, for the moment, with his nervous system. (But the world is all before me, mine to choose, and my doctor knows much more about my nervous system than I do: he, not I, can distinguish between steady, efficient functioning, and euphoria!) In a very interesting interview in Ian Hamilton's *the Review* Empson, I remember, said he could not now accept the argument of this very fine poem; it was too much an Oscar Wilde argument, a let's-pretend argument, and much as there is to be said for good old Oscar,

> *The Duchess she was dressing,*
> *Dressing for the ball,*
> *When there she saw old Oscar*
> *A-standing by the wall . . .*

Empson did not want to be a Wildean, saying that only deliberate pretence and projection of imaginary meanings will give any sense to the meaningless of the universe. Empson, in this great poem, as I think it, mentions Wittgenstein:

> *What is conceivable can happen too,*
> *Said Wittgenstein, who had not dreamt of you . . .*

For Wittgenstein, in the *Tractatus*, the world was simply everything that was the case, an endless accumulation of atomic facts, which are facts about inconceivably simple entities. (A blue spot on a white wall cannot, for instance, be a constituent of an atomic fact, since it is both extended and coloured, and exists in an extended and coloured spatial context: Wittgenstein had invented a wonderful slotting machine, into which nothing conceivable, since we cannot imagine an absolutely simple particular, could slot. But the world was this set of slots, anyway, with whatever unimaginable simples they contained. And the meaning of the world, 'the mystical', lay outside the world, and since it could not be conceived clearly ought not to be spoken about. I imagine that Wittgenstein, whose favourite reading was American pulp thriller magazines like The Black Mask, never read poetry, and had never considered poetry's round-about way of saying things.)**

Empson, I think, dislikes philosophers on the whole, as many poets do: but to have intellectually matured in that extraordinarily distinguished Cambridge of the 1920s, when Richards and Wittgenstein and Moore were around (and the young Leavis, to be sure, but I do not think that Empson ever took much of an impact from Leavis), must have left its mark on him. Most really fine poets know and do not really know what they know, can say things they did not think they were going to say; from quarter of an hour's casual browsing in a library, may have constructed, and forgotten, a whole system of philosophy. Empson's mind is, in a sense, the opposite of philosophical. I think the beautifully tedious prose of G. E. Moore, leaving no possible step in an argument out, fussing and fretting over every even faintly ambiguous concept sublimely pedestrian, one might say, is the model of what a good philosopher's prose should be: whereas Empson's mind, in prose or verse, moves in seven-league boots, in a giant's elliptical leaps, and there are great Serbonian bogs between his premises and his conclusions. But Cambridge, in his time there, was a great philosophical place, and this must have influenced him: an influence, as Empson himself said of that of T. S. Eliot, bleak and penetrating, like an east wind. I remember, and perhaps retain, the agony of my own youth enough to still feel the impact of the early poems very strongly. The state of youthfulness is a state of soaring aspiration blocked and thwarted by the blockishness of people and things: as Shakespeare's Troilus says:

> This is the monstruositie in love Lady, that the will is infinite, and the execution confined; that the desire is boundless and the act a slave to limit.

That is what the earlier poems seem to me to be about, and love can be love of the divine, a fable, and the lady in a love poem can be a poetic fiction. Marvell's Coy Mistress, all the modern critics seem to agree, never existed (he settled down, after the Restoration, to a very humdrum liaison with his landlady). The poem is in a convention, or it plays brilliantly with a convention: but Marvell's feelings about death, pleasure, and frustration were, I think, like the young Empson's, real enough.

The Gathering Storm of 1940 (it is one of Empson's often repeated but perpetually good jokes to claim that Winston Churchill, for an early volume of his Second World War memoirs, cribbed without acknowledgment Empson's title) is quite different. Empson was teaching in Japan between 1931 and 1934, in Tokyo National University, and between 1937 and 1939 in the National University at Peking. I suppose the intervening period in England may have been largely taken up with arranging for the publication of both *Poems* and *Some Versions of Pastoral* in 1935. And in seeing old friends. There is an astonishing new social maturity of tone, a sense of what history is like, a refusal to be either panicky or utopian: he knew that we were in for a bad time, in these islands, but felt that we would get through it. In China, in the later 1930s, he had been caught up in the Great March, or the Great Retreat, from the invading Japanese and had given his lessons in various remote places, relying on his extraordinary memory for verse he had read (prose is harder to remember, but he does say in one poem that he had memorized a paragraph by Virginia Woolf) and on the blackboard. Far Eastern education does consist very largely of memorialization. There is a system of deference, the Confucian system, and a rather more rigid pecking order between different grades of lecturer than our British universities allow, but on the other hand Japanese and Chinese students will not respect a *sensei* unless they respect him morally, feel that, teaching and embodying order, he has created order in himself. I have taught in Japan myself: on various visits to Sheffield, it has often struck me that, not only by his colleagues and his students, but by the waitresses in the Senior Common Room or by barmen and barwomen in pubs, he is treated with the kind of deference accorded in Japan to the *sensei*, who is expected to be not a mere instructor or expert but a sort of sage. Like King Lear, Empson has authority in his eye; and in his remote and brusque way, he has a great deal of warmth: on my last visit to Sheffield I was very much amused and touched by a conversation between a waitress and William about a special number of a university magazine, which had included both a tribute to him by students, and a little piece by himself. The waitress was saying how deserved the tribute was; William was saying that his own contribution was rather a hasty piece of work. Neither at a surface level was quite taking in what the other was saying, they were at semantic cross-purposes, but one felt that they were at one with each other, were making the right warm noises to each other, in a way that made semantics comparatively unimportant. Restricted codes, on both sides, made possible an intimacy that elaborated codes often preclude.

It seems silly to talk about restricted codes in

connection with such an acknowledgedly difficult poet. But in writing, as in life, Empson often says brief, gruff things, which you must pick up at once if at all, for expansion and elaboration would destroy them. The restricted code implies, flatteringly, that the reader or interlocutor is, in Conrad's phrase, 'one of us'. In this sense, I go back to *The Gathering Storm* often, for what I can only call wisdom. I am by nature touchy, resentful, and liable to harbour grudges for a long time. Remembering a line and a half from a fine and patriotic poem in *The Gathering Storm*,

> As to be hurt is petty, and to be hard
> Stupidity . . .

has very often, if not often enough, helped me to check back these disagreeable tendencies in my nature. I find myself also remembering lines, apparently flippant or frivolous, for their condensed truth:

> For every style comes down to noise,

or one, about a Japanese train in Manchuria, which fascinated the young John Wain:

> For I, a twister, love what I abhor,

One would not, perhaps, call Empson a philosophical poet: simply because he would never sacrifice a genuine insight, however it might seem to contradict the general directions in which his thought and life move, to a desire to appear consistent and systematic. But I would call him a wise poet. And yet wisdom is not enough. Wordsworth's *The Excursion* is a wise poem but a lot of it is flat stuff that takes a lot of plodding through. Empson's restricted poetic code, in the sense in which I have been using the phrase, leads to an off-hand elegance, a tart concision. His poems have something almost like a physical savour; 'a taste in the head'.

William Empson
Routledge

---

* Died April 1975. She was just 27 and to my mind the most exciting poet and critic of her generation.

** I am unjust to Wittgenstein. Leavis has described him construing a difficult early poem of Empson's brilliantly.

> *The words of a dead man*
> *Are modified in the guts of the living.*

It is necessary to say at once that my attitude to-
wards Auden's poetry is deeply divided on certain
fundamental issues. For that reason, this essay can-
not be straightforward appreciation, or a basic in-
troduction, despite its very limited scope. It is
intended, rather, as an exploration of Auden's atti-
tude towards England, as it is manifested in his
work, particularly in its early phase, and as a for-
mative influence on the nature of that work. It must
also be, in some respects, a rather querulous
appraisal, equivocal in its praise. Yet, what I under-
stand by reverence for an author usually takes one
of two forms: either total assent to the central im-
portance of his writing, known as an influence in the
reader's life, or a questioning, even quarrelsome,
engagement with it, also known as such an influence,
but an ambiguous one. If to this latter form, which
my attitude to Auden's poetry takes, I add that for
more than a decade I have found lines and whole
poems by him associated with my feelings and
thoughts, then it may explain why I risk writing on
this subject now, and why I think of it as an expres-
sion of gratitude.

I

'Very soon, it seems, they will be labelling authors,
like automobiles, by the year. Already the decade
classification is absurd, for it suggests that authors
conveniently stop writing at the age of thirty-five or
so.' Of course, Auden was right to criticize the crude
forms of classification that most critics adopt, at
one time or another, when more concerned to label
an author than to enter fully into his work. Right,
too, when he wrote: 'When a writer is dead, one

ought to be able to see that his various works, taken together, make one consistent *oeuvre*.' Yet it is inevitable that the reader should often isolate one phase of a writer's development as the one he prefers, though whether he is then justified in describing it as the essential one, is another question entirely. For me, by far the most interesting phase of Auden's writing ended with the publication of *Another Time* in 1940, and is represented mainly by *Poems* (1930), *The Orators* (1932), *Look, Stranger!* (1936), and the plays written in collaboration with Christopher Isherwood. I believe, however, that his work, from *Paid on Both Sides* (1930) to *Epistle to a godson* (1972), does constitute 'one consistent *oeuvre*' – one that is uneven throughout and in which *Homage to Clio* (1960) is the last collection that can be described as in any sense major, but which embodies a single, developing, imaginative commitment to an idea of poetry, and to certain attitudes, materials, beliefs. There are also poems in the later collections (*Nones, The Shield of Achilles* and *Homage to Clio*), and passages in the longer poems, which I find as admirable, or more so, than the best of the earlier work. For instance, it seems to me that nowhere has he written with more epigrammatic force, compassion and authority than in 'The Shield of Achilles' itself. The following stanzas evoke the scene of the Crucifixion, placed in a modern but universally human context, as it appears on the shield:

Barbed wire enclosed an arbitrary spot
Where bored officials lounged (one cracked a joke)
And sentries sweated for the day was hot:
A crowd of ordinary decent folk
Watched from without and neither moved nor spoke
As three pale figures were led forth and bound
To three posts driven upright in the ground.

> The mass and majesty of this world, all
>> That carries weight and always weighs the same
> Lay in the hands of others; they were small
>> And could not hope for help and no help came:
> What their foes liked to do was done, their
>> shame
> Was all the world could wish; they lost their pride
>> And died as men before their bodies died.

Characteristically, the changing scenes on the shield, now suggested in their broad aspect, now seen in an emblematic detail, occur in what are primarily moral settings, where man acts out his condition, viewed from above. This technique Auden developed in his attempt to diagnose the condition of English society in the thirties. But, although diagnosis is a necessary word to use when speaking of Auden, throughout his work the diagnostician is conscious of being infected by the sickness he prescribes for and observes.

Of himself at Oxford in the mid-twenties, Auden wrote, in *Letter to Lord Byron*:

> A raw provincial, my good taste was tardy,
>> And Edward Thomas I as yet preferred;

> I was still listening to Thomas Hardy
>> Putting divinity about a bird;
>> But Eliot spoke the still unspoken word;
> For gasworks and dried tubers I forsook
> The clock at Grantchester, the English rook.

True to the style of this often very witty poem, in its least witty passages, the comment here is slightly revealing but almost wholly superficial. In the thirties Auden did indeed make use of an imagery suggested by 'gasworks and dried tubers', surface features of *The Waste Land*, but derived nothing essential either from Eliot or the other great modernists, Pound and Joyce. By the essentials of modernism I mean principles of organization, methods of juxtaposing apparently disparate scenes on the basis of a common archetypal pattern, as in *The Waste Land* and *Ulysses*, and of embodying the past in the present and setting the present in the context of the past. Where Auden uses Joycean techniques, as in parts of *The Orators*, or echoes Eliot, he derives mainly from the surface of their work, from the appearance of their forms and from stylistic mannerisms. Not that *The Orators* is entirely imitative, but it is, as Auden's most self-consciously modernist work, one that combines mimicry of various other writers' styles with distinctly personal preoccupations, rather than a convincing fusion of its electic manners and original matter. This is another way of saying that Auden's poetry was only ever modernist in appearance – a fact that will be held against him only by those who belittle the alternative traditions still vital in this century. Without maintaining this extreme position, I would still argue that Auden's disregard of the essentials of modernism obstructed his attempt to write a completely convincing long poem, convincing that is as an integrated whole, unifying content and form. It seems to me that all his longer poems, despite superficial ingenuities, and with the exception of *Paid on Both Sides*, are fundamentally discursive. All can be paraphrased in a way that, for example, *The Waste Land* and *The Anathemata* cannot. In other words, he organises his material – his ideas – on an essentially prosaic basis, and the pleasure his longer poems afford is intellectual, not imaginative: we apprehend the ideas, wittily or idiosyncratically expressed, with the intellect, but in *The Waste Land* different levels of meaning, image echoing image, affect consciousness at a level at which what is experienced cannot be described in other words. The variety within Auden's longer poems, especially *New*

30

Year Letter and *The Age of Anxiety*, is effected by the range from dramatic speech and lyricism to doggerel: we are being talked to, now brilliantly or movingly, now awkwardly. It matters, of course, what the talk is about – that it often touches intimately, instructively, on questions of first importance – but in my view such a discursive method solves none of the problems of the long poem. Even *Paid on Both Sides*, with its dramatic form, can be appreciated without much loss as a number of concentrated, lyrical passages removed from context.

It is anything but my intention to level these criticisms at Auden's adoption, from the start, of the comic spirit, or his refusal (after a distinctly oratorical beginning) of the bardic role. The criticisms centre entirely on the discursive nature of much of his work. On the other hand, in many of those poems which he called *Songs and Other Musical Pieces*, to my ear Auden is next to Yeats the finest lyrical poet since Tennyson. There are other forms of verbal music than those to be found in, for example, 'As I walked out one Evening', 'Lay your sleeping head, my love', 'Lady, weeping at the crossroads', 'Look, stranger, on this island now', 'If I Could Tell You', but at any time, and especially when prosaic spirits with no sense of rhythm of any kind can set up as poets, Auden's lyrical gift would be something to be profoundly grateful for. Also, when all has been said about his apparently changing allegiances, in how many other poets does one find, expressed so movingly, an equivalent deep compassion for the displaced peoples of Hitler's Europe, to that of 'Refugee Blues'? It would make no sense for me to write about Auden even in a limited way without acknowledging how moving as well as entertaining I find poems as different from each other in form as 'Roman Wall Blues' and 'In Praise of Limestone'.

II

If Auden owed nothing that was essential to T. S. Eliot, his deeper affinities in the thirties were, I believe, with Hardy and Edward Thomas, to whom he was so condescending in *Letter to Lord Byron*. More broadly speaking, instead of making use of Eliot's formal innovations Auden developed several lines from that alternative tradition, as it is often called now, which comprises elements from many centuries of English poetry – from Anglo-Saxon elegy and Middle English love song and meditative poem, from the ballads and the Elizabethan dramatic lyric, from the romantic movement and its Victorian heirs – and descends to us, modified, in the highly individual but traditional voices of such poets as Hardy, Edward Thomas and Wilfred Owen. (I do not mean, of course, that all the elements referred to are to be found in each of these poets, only that they formed the language, instincts, and conceptions of poetry from which they wrote.) In *Poems* (1930) several elements of this complex tradition are fused, not the least apparent being a deep feeling for landscape and the inanimate which is akin to what we find in Hardy and Edward Thomas. In my view, the common ground of feeling, embodied in landscape, is a peculiarly inward apprehension of death, known in the self, in the English countryside and in nature at large. Although such feeling can be discerned in a great deal of English poetry – probably in all poetry, since death is necessarily one of the primary themes – in Edward Thomas, for example, it was augmented by the sense, intimate as breathing, of living in a society in decline, of failing faith in those powers of renewal traditionally embodied, or symbolized, by the natural world. In fact, I believe it was not only a society in decline, but a dying culture, rooted in the natural world, that influenced the death-haunted poetry of Hardy as well as of Edward Thomas. And it was a similar feeling which Auden inherited, not only from reading them but from his birth and up-bringing in pre-war and wartime England. Not exactly in *the* England of these poets, of course, any more than their Englands were identical – too many questions of class, time, and locality arise to allow such an abstraction. Nevertheless, what I believe all had in common was their primal attachment to a world with no potentiality for growth or renewal, no future that did not entail an uncreative return to the past. Eliot too was a death-haunted poet, but for him there was surely no basic experience, in quite that way, of discovering how equivocal was the object of his love, and when he did return to the past it was to the now and always, the pattern of timeless moments.

The sense of doom that shadows Auden's poetry of the thirties obviously derived as much from memories of the First World War as from the slide towards the Second. The war games and sense of guilt prevalent in the poetry of this period derived in part, just as obviously, from the fantasies of a boy who had watched young men of the previous generation being asked to die, and dying, for their country. It is hardly surprising, then, that there should be a good deal of inverted patriotism – or half-inverted patriotism, still equivocal, still attached to the rejected sentiments – in Auden's early verse. This can be seen in the skill with which he mimics the rhetoric of Patriotism in *The Orators* or in *Paid on Both Sides*:

> I know we have and are making terrific sacrifices, but we cannot give in. We cannot betray the dead. As we pass their graves can we be deaf to the simple eloquence of their inscriptions, those who in the glory of their early manhood gave up their lives for us? No, we must fight to the finish.

The confluent influences of Freud (more potently,

33

Groddeck) and Marx on early Auden have been examined by many critics, who have also considered those central figures the spy, the exile and the airman, showing how the diseased bourgeois intellectual is at once inside and outside his doomed class, an agent of the life-force who bears the death-wish in his own person. The complex but coherent dramatization of this predicament, set in a glacial northern landscape with remnants of dead industry, and abandoned mines, provided the singular atmospheric unity of *Poems*. There, Auden or his persona, 'tiny observer of enormous world', is obsessed with the sacrificial death:

> You whom I gladly walk with, touch
> Or wait for as one certain of good,
> We know it, we know that love
> Needs more than the admiring excitement of
>   union,
> More than the abrupt self-confident farewell,
> The heel on the finishing blade of grass,
> The self-confidence of the falling root,
> Needs death, death of the grain, our death,
> Death of the old gang.

Rendered with more or less subtlety and power, the sacrificial feeling dominates *Poems* and recurs, in an increasingly discursive form, in *Look, Stranger!* To some readers, no doubt the feeling seems hopelessly bourgeois or adolescent. It is certainly more exciting to feel doomed in one's twenties than at any later time, and perhaps it is only then that enormous satisfaction can be gained from chanting to one's friends—

> Seekers after happiness, all who follow
> The convolutions of your simple wish,
> It is later than you think; nearer that day
> Far other than that distant afternoon

34

> *Amid rustle of frocks and stamping feet*
> *They gave the prizes to the ruined boys.*
> *You cannot be away, then, no*
> *Not though you pack to leave within an hour,*
> *Escaping humming down arterial roads:*
> *The date was yours; the prey to fugues,*
> *Irregular breathing and alternate ascendancies*
> *After some haunted migratory years*
> *To disintegrate on an instant in the explosion of*
> *   mania*
> *Or lapse for ever into a classic fatigue.*

As for adolesence, though, quite a lot of Keats's major poetry appeals directly to that much maligned, but essential stage of growth. And Auden's poetry of doom surely expresses a genuine sense of torment, not of a class alone, or the poet alone, but of all, whatever their origins, who are conscious of being part of a death-haunted, and apparently death-willing, society.

Elsewhere I have tried to show that Edward Thomas wrote primarily from the experience of internalized crisis, haunted by his awareness of how much around him, in the English countryside he loved, was dying and by the presence in himself of that death. It is of vital significance, then, to note how in the thirties, for all his talk of 'gasworks and dried tubers', Auden set poem after poem in English landscapes – often against Pennine limestone or other northern uplands, where recent human occupation is evident in its industrial remains. Auden's success in evoking this type of landscape should make us aware of his affinities with Hardy and Edward Thomas, but also, I believe, of the kind of poet he might have become:

> *Who stands, the crux left of the watershed,*
> *On the wet road between the chafing grass*
> *Below him sees dismantled washing-floors,*

Snatches of tramline running to the wood,
An industry already comatose,
Yet sparsely living. A ramshackle engine
At Cashwell raises water; for ten years
It lay in flooded workings until this,
Its latter office, grudgingly performed,
And further here and there, though many dead
Lie under the poor soil, some acts are chosen
Taken from recent winters; two there were
Cleaned out a damaged shaft by hand, clutching
The winch the gale would tear them from; one died
During a storm, the fells impassable,
Not at his village, but in wooden shape
Through long abandoned levels nosed his way
And in his final valley went to ground.

A single place-name is hardly sufficient evidence on which to hang a theory of affinities, but the place itself is rendered lovingly enough to remind us of Hardy and Thomas, especially when we consider that 'many dead lie under the poor soil'. But Auden's rendering of the landscape does not, ostensibly, embody a special relationship between poet and place, but creates a dramatic metaphor for the condition of England. It is also an industrial, humanized landscape, as those of the other poets are rural landscapes enriched by personal and historical associations. Yet, surely, there is enough evidence in this one stanza of Auden's attraction to the inanimate? On one level, this is a love poem which celebrates its small world of inanimate objects, where the machines are really elemental. In fact, the feeling invested in these objects is as primal as any found in Hardy's Wessex. Moreover, Auden may well have thought Wordsworth 'a most bleak old bore', but there is also at least a touch of Wordsworth about his rendering of the inanimate.

'It is from the sacred encounters of his imagination that a poet's impulse to write a poem arises. Thanks to the language, he need not name them directly unless he wishes; he can describe one in terms of another and translate those that are private or irrational or socially unacceptable into such as are acceptable to reason and society. Every poem he writes involves his whole past. Every love poem, for instance, is hung with trophies of lovers gone, and among these may be some very peculiar objects indeed. The lovely lady of the present may number among her predecessors an overshot waterwheel.' It is my belief that the primary sacred encounter of Auden's imagination was with objects and a landscape akin to those evoked in the poem quoted above. Indeed, he seems to tell us so clearly enough when this statement at the end of his lecture *Making, Knowing and Judging*, together with his affirmation that 'every poem is rooted in imaginative awe', recalls its beginning. There, in speaking of his childhood's 'private world of Sacred Objects', he is obviously referring to such inanimates – machines and minerals – as those described in such books as *Underground Life, Machinery for Metalliferous Mines* and *Lead and Zinc Ores of Northumberland and Alston Moor*. Given such an understandable and attractive imaginative bias, it is not surprising, nevertheless, that it should come into conflict with awareness of human responsibility and his abiding preoccupation with Love, later Eros and Agape. Not surprising that resistance to such a world of sacred objects, and translation of his feelings for it into other terms, should include resistance to a loved landscape and even to nature itself. Further proof of Auden's attraction to the non-human world is provided by the strength of his need to counter it, so that a dominant, even an obsessive, theme of the later poetry contrasts the human world of consciousness and responsibility with the unconscious, creaturely or natural world. Furthermore, in the early poetry the lapse back into the unconsciousness of matter is a theme that provokes strong feelings of attraction and repulsion. For instance, John Nower, in *Paid on Both Sides*, experiences the temptation in an acute form:

> Could I have been some simpleton that lived
> Before disaster sent his runners here;
> Younger than worms, worms have too much to
>   bear.
> Yes, mineral were best: could I but see
> These woods, these fields of green, this lively
>   world
> Sterile as moon.

The Chorus echoes his sentiments:

> Better where no one feels,
> The out-of-sight, buried too deep for shafts.

The limestone landscape, which is like the tip of an iceberg, is often, throughout the poetry, associated or even identified with the mother, in the form of life's unconscious matrix. It is this to which the 'tiny observer', conscious that social renewal requires the destruction of his class, is tempted to turn in his intolerable predicament. Exile and airman, in working out their strategies for curing the diseased society of which they are infected parts, are tempted by the lapse into unconsciousness. It is a complex theme with which Auden is concerned, expressed in psychological and social terms that are sometimes at variance. Yet the urgency of feeling in these poems is unmistakable, and it often centres on the need to escape a maternal influence identified with the ruined, non-human world. The child's birth in *Paid on Both Sides* is precipitated by his father's

38

violent death; it is the mothers on each side who keep the feud alive, so that, finally, 'his mother and her mother won'. Naturally, both psychologically and socially the mother can be seen to symbolize a great deal, but I am convinced that the maternal figure also symbolizes that buried world which was the object of the poet's first love, and which now tempts him to resolve an intolerable situation by escaping into it.

I am arguing, then, that Auden's translation of this feeling into psychological and social terms, and his resistance to it, provided a great deal of the creative pressure for *Poems*. Moreover, that in his poetry of the thirties, in his most self-evidently English phase, he lived through, reflected, and in one way resolved a general crisis of feeling about England, which was then (and still is to some extent) both a capitalist imperial power and the locality known in childhood. He did not turn towards celebration of an English landscape or locality, because for him that dominant theme of the tradition which he inherited was a dangerous form of escapism. Instead, he sought to understand the society as a whole, viewing it from some high place, like the Malverns, that was both actual and symbolic, physically in England but above English society, or from the vantage point of hawk or airman. In doing so, he developed a rhetoric that is alternatively exciting in its power to suggest a society seen at large, but known in physical and diagnostic detail, or distasteful in its condescension. Thus, addressing Love in the 'Prologue' to *Look, Stranger!*, he wrote:

> Here too on our little reef display your power,
> This fortress perched on the edge of the Atlantic
>   scarp,
> The mole between all Europe and the exile-
>   crowded sea;

And make us as Newton *was who, in his garden*
watching
The apple falling towards England, *became aware*
Between himself and her of an eternal tie.

For now that dream which so long had contented
our will,
I mean, of uniting the dead into a splendid empire,
Under whose fertilizing flood the Lancashire *moss*

Sprouted up chimneys, and Glamorgan *hid a life*
Grim as a tidal rock-pool's in its glove-shaped
valleys,
Is already retreating into her maternal shadow;

Leaving the furnaces gasping in the impossible air,
That flotsam at which Dumbarton *gapes and*
hungers;
While upon wind-loved Rowley *no hammer shakes*

The cluster of mounds like a midget golf-course,
graves
Of some who created these intelligible dangerous
marvels,
Affectionate people, but crude their sense of glory.

For the most part, these names are not numinous,
sacred from their association with childhood places,
but belong to a Britain spread out like a map – a
peculiarly Audenesque map which denotes and diag-
noses the sickness of the places it names. Such a
view was one valid response to the question posed in
The Orators: 'What do you think about England,
this country of ours where nobody is well?', and to
the crucial awareness of how easily an idolator of
sacred objects might be absorbed into the 'maternal
shadow'.

Shortly after the turn of the decade, Auden, resi-
dent in New York, discoursed about some of the
pressures formative of his powerful early verse, in-
directly, in *New Year Letter*:

> Whenever I begin to think
> About the human creature we
> Must nurse to sense and decency,
> An English area comes to mind,
> I see the nature of my kind
> As a locality I love,
> Those limestone moors that stretch from
> > BROUGH
> To HEXHAM and the ROMAN WALL,
> There is my symbol of us all.

A place which has become 'my symbol of us all' is no longer accessory to a 'private world of Sacred Objects'; instead of tempting the idolator, it offers a landscape symbolic of man's faulty nature. The fault is now fallen man's, no longer merely the sickness of English society. To Auden now, England is 'my own tongue,/ And what I did when I was young'. The exile with whom many of the earlier poems was concerned has stepped out of the maternal shadow and become the quester, who believes:

> However we decide to act,
> Decision must accept the fact
> That the machine has now destroyed
> The local customs we enjoyed,
> Replaced the bonds of blood and nation
> By personal confederation.
> No longer can we learn our good
> From chances of a neighbourhood
> Or class or party, or refuse
> As individuals to choose
> Our loves, authorities, and friends,
> To judge our means and plan our ends;
> For the machine has cried aloud
> And publicized among the crowd
> The secret that was always true
> But known once only to the few,
> Compelling all to the admission,
> Aloneness is man's real condition,

That each must travel forth alone
In search of the Essential Stone,
'The Nowhere-without-No' that is
The justice of societies.

The advantage, as it may also be one of the defects, of discursive poetry is that the reader can always answer back. Aloneness may, or may not, be 'man's real condition'. One could say, it all depends on the man. It is equally possible to maintain that Auden's idea of 'local customs', 'bonds of blood and nation', and 'neighbourhood' was over-influenced by a middle-class version of English society. Certainly, its portrayal in *The Orators* and *The Dog Beneath the Skin* – indeed, in his work as a whole – convinces me that this was so and that he knew little of what many people still experience as rootedness, though they do not necessarily idealize those roots or falsify them in any other way. Yet it also seems to me that Auden's development was completely honest, and that he did survive one form of sickness inherent in the society and always liable to infect a poet's feeling for English landscape and his childhood idols. If it entailed a loss of intensity, then far better his lonely, compassionate quest than the Georgians' unawareness of the true nature of the dream of Old England with which they were infatuated. Of course, England in its changing countryside, suburbs and cities still remains to be known in depth; others have other ways of humanizing their sacred objects, or find them sacred precisely because they are non-human; but Auden's was one way, a way of rooting himself in the modern rootless experience that was not an escape, but courageous, intellectually honest, and true to the love he consistently invoked.

Poetry Wales

Irving Howe   **The Plath Celebration**
               A Partial Dissent

I

A glamour of fatality hangs over the name of Sylvia
Plath, the glamour that has made her a darling of
our culture. Extremely gifted, her will clenched into
a fist of ambition, several times driven to suicide by
a suffering so absolute as to seem almost imper-
sonal, yet in her last months composing poems in
which pathology and clairvoyance triumphantly fuse
– these are the materials of her legend. It is a legend
that solicits our desires for a heroism of sickness
that can serve as emblem of the age, and many
young readers take in Sylvia Plath's vibrations of
despair as if they were the soul's own oxygen. For
reasons good and bad, the spokesmen for the sen-
sibility of extreme gesture – all the blackness, con-
fession, denial, and laceration that are warranted by
modern experience but are also the moral bromides
of our moment – see in Sylvia Plath an authentic
priestess. Because she is authentic, the role would
surely displease her; dead now for a decade, she can
offer no defense.

Quantities of adoring criticism pile up around her,
composed in a semi-mimetic frenzy designed to be
equivalent in tone to its subject. The result is poor
criticism, worse prose. In a collection of essays de-
voted to Sylvia Plath, the editor writes – almost as if
he too were tempted by an oven: 'The courting of
experience that kills is characteristic of major
poets.'[1] Is it? Virgil, Petrarch, Goethe, Pope, Hugo,
Wordsworth, Bialik, Yeats, Stevens, Auden, Frost?

In dissenting a little from the Plath celebration,
one has the sense not so much of disagreeing about
the merits of certain poems as of plunging into a
harsh *kulturkampf*. For one party in this struggle

[1] *The Art of Sylvia Plath*, edited by Charles Newman
(Indiana University Press).

43

Sylvia Plath has become an icon, and the dangers for those in the other party are also considerable, since it would be unjust to allow one's irritation with her devotees to spill over into one's response to her work. So let us move quickly to the facts about her career and then to the poems she wrote toward the end of her life, crucial for any judgment of her work.

Her father, a professor of biology and (it's important to note) a man of German descent, died when she was nine. The reverberations of this event are heavy in the poems, though its precise significance for Sylvia Plath as either person or poet is very hard to grasp. She then lived with her mother in Wellesley, Massachusetts; she went to Smith, an ardent student who swept up all the prizes; she suffered from psychic disorders; she won a Fullbright to Cambridge University, then met and married a gifted English poet, Ted Hughes. In 1960 she published her first book of poems, *The Colossus* – it rings with distinguished echoes, proclaims unripe gifts, contains more quotable passages than successful poems (true for all her work). She had two children, in 1960 and 1962, to whom she seems to have been fiercely attached and about whom she wrote some of her better poems. She was separated from her husband, lived one freezing winter in London with her children, and, experiencing an onslaught of energy at once overwhelming and frightening, wrote her best-known poems during the last weeks of her life. On February 11, 1963, she killed herself.

Crossing the Water contains some of the poems she wrote between the early work of *The Colossus* and the final outburst that would appear posthumously in 1965 as *Ariel*. There are graphic lines in *Crossing the Water*, but few poems fully achieved. 'The desert is white as a blind man's eye,/ Comfortless as salt . . .' we read in a poem not otherwise notable. The drive to self-destruction that would

tyrannize the last poems is already at work in these
'middle' ones:

> *If I pay the roots of the heather*
> *Too close attention, they will invite me*
> *To whiten my bones among them.*

The poems in *Crossing the Water* are, neverthe-
less, more open in voice and variable in theme than
those for which Sylvia Plath has become famous;
they have less power but also less pathology. She
writes well, in snatches and stanzas, about the im-
personal moments of personal experience, when the
sense of everything beyond one's selfhood dominates
the mind. She writes well, that is, precisely about
the portion of human experience that is most absent
in the *Ariel* poems; such poems as 'Parliament Hill
Fields', 'Small Hours', and a few others in *Crossing
the Water*, unheroic in temper and unforced in pitch,
can yield familiar pleasures. The flaws in her work
she describes charmingly in 'Stillborn', though it's
characteristic that, after the vivid opening stanza,
the poem should itself seem stillborn:

> *These poems do not live: it's a sad diagnosis.*
> *They grew their toes and fingers well enough,*
> *Their little foreheads bulged with concentration.*
> *If they missed out on walking about like people*
> *It wasn't for any lack of mother love.*

II

At a crucial point in her career Sylvia Plath came
under the influence of Robert Lowell's *Life Studies*,
and it is this relationship that has led many admirers
to speak of her late work as 'confessional poetry.'
The category is interesting but dubious, both in
general and when applied to Sylvia Plath.

In *Life Studies* Lowell broke into a new style. He
abandoned the complex interlacings of idea and

image, the metaphysical notations and ironic turnings of his earlier work, and instead wrote poems that were to deal immediately with his own experience: his time as CO, his nervous breakdowns, his relations with his wife. When he wrote 'I' it was clear he really did mean his private self, not a *persona* created for the poem's occasion. To the small number of people who read poetry at all, *Life Studies* came as a valued, perhaps overvalued, shock – a harsh abandonment of the Eliotian impersonality that had previously dominated American poetry. Inevitably, this new style was widely imitated and its inherent difficulty frequently ignored. The readiness with which Lowell exposed his own life caused people to admire his courage rather than scrutinize his poems. Candor was raised to an absolute value, such as it need not often be in either morals or literature. Our culture was then starting to place an enormous stress on self-exposure, self-assault, self-revelation – as if spontaneity were a sure warrant of authenticity, and spilling out a sure road to comprehension. The bared breast replaced the active head.

Insofar as a poem depends mainly on the substance of its confession, as blow or shock revealing some hidden shame in the writer's experience, it will rarely be a first-rate piece of work. It will lack the final composure that even the most excited composition requires. Insofar as it makes the confessional element into something integral to the poem, it ceases, to that extent, to be confessional. It becomes a self-sufficient poem, not dependent for its value on whatever experience may have evoked it. Perhaps the greatest achievement of this kind in English is the group of poems Thomas Hardy wrote in 1912–13 after the death of his first wife: they are full of the regrets of wasted life, missed opportunities, shamed quarrels, but they take on an autonomous life, beyond the rawness of confession.

Now, this is dogma and, as such, suspect – even

by those who may agree with it. For obviously there are cases where residues of personal confession can be detected, yet the poem constitutes more than a mere notation of incident or memory. I would also add that the short lyric is a form likely to resist confessional writing, since it does not allow for the sustained moral complication, the full design of social or historical setting, that can transform confession from local act to larger meaning. The confessions of Augustine and Rousseau are long works, and they are in prose.

A flaw in confessional poetry, even the best of it, is one that characterizes much other American poetry in the twentieth century. It is the notion that a careful behavioral notation of an event or object is in itself sufficient basis for composing a satisfactory poem: the description of an orange, a wheelbarrow, a woman's gait. What such poems depend on, for their very life, is the hope of creating an aura, a network of implication, that will enlarge the scope of their references. Sometimes, as in Frost's 'Spring Pools', this feat is managed; too often, what we get is a mere verbal snapshot, a discrete instance, that has little reverberation. And this holds true even if the snapshot records an event that rouses our curiosity or dismay.

Robert Lowell's poem, 'Man and Wife', shook many readers when it first appeared in 1952. When you read a poem that begins—

Tamed by Miltown, we lie on Mother's bed;
the rising sun in war paint dyes us red;
in broad daylight her gilded bedposts shine,
abandoned, almost Dionysian.

—some feeling of involvement, even pain, is likely to be invoked through the very announcement of its subject. There is the compressed suggestibility of 'Mother's bed', the vividness of the 'war paint' in the second line. But the poem as a whole no longer seems quite so remarkable as I once thought. In the middle – and the middle is where confessional poems get into trouble, once the subject has been declared and something must now be *done* with it – Lowell declines into a recollection about the time he 'outdrank the Rahvs in the heat/ Of Greenwich Village.' Most readers do not know 'the Rahvs', and the reference is therefore lost upon them; those few who do may find it possible to resist the poet's intention. Here the poem has slipped into self-indulgence. At the end, Lowell does achieve a recovery with several lines describing his wife's invective after a quarrel, presumably before Miltown 'tamed' them both:

> *your old-fashioned tirade—*
> *loving, rapid, merciless—*
> *breaks like the Atlantic Ocean on my head.*

These lines move the center of the poem away from the confessing, preening self of the poet and reveal a counteraction: that's not just a prop lying there in bed with him, it's another human being. True, the reference remains local and thereby, perhaps, open to the kind of criticism I made earlier of confessional poetry as a whole. But through severe detail Lowell has managed to suggest reverberations that move the poem beyond the edges of his personal wound.

At times Sylvia Plath also wrote confessional poetry, as in the much-praised 'Lady Lazarus', a poem about her recurrent suicide attempts. Its opening lines, like almost all her opening lines, come at one like a driven hammer:

> *I have done it again.*
> *One year in every ten*
> *I manage it—*

48

> A sort of walking miracle, my skin
> Bright as a Nazi lampshade,
> My right foot
>
> A paperweight,
> My face a featureless, fine
> Jew linen.

The tone is jeeringly tough, but at least partly directed against herself. There is a strain of self-irony ('a sort of walking miracle') such as poetry of this kind can never have enough of. Still, one must be infatuated with the Plath legend to ignore the poet's need for enlarging the magnitude of her act through illegitimate comparisons with the Holocaust (a point to which I will return later).

Sylvia Plath's most notable gift as a writer – a gift for the single, isolate image – comes through later in the poem when, recalling an earlier suicide attempt, she writes that they had to 'pick the worms off me like sticky pearls.' But then, after patching together some fragments of recollection, she collapses into an archness about her suicide attempts that is shocking in a way she could not have intended:

> I do it so it feels like hell.
> I do it so it feels real.
> I guess you could say I've a call.
>
> It's easy enough to do it in a cell,
> It's easy enough to do it and stay put.

As if uneasy about the tone of such lines, she then drives toward what I can only see as a willed hysteric tone, the forcing of language to make up for an inability to develop the matter. The result is sentimental violence:

49

> *A cake of soap,*
> *A wedding ring.*
> *A gold filling. . . .*
>
> *Out of the ash*
> *I rise with my red hair*
> *And I eat men like air.*

In the end, the several remarkable lines in this poem serve only to intensify its badness, for in their isolation, without the support of a rational structure, they leave the author with no possibility of development other than violent wrenchings in tone. And this is a kind of badness that seems a constant temptation in confessional poetry, the temptation to reveal all with one eye nervously measuring the effect of revelation.

There's another famous poem by Sylvia Plath entitled, 'Cut', in which she shows the same mixture of strong phrasing and structural incoherence. 'Cut' opens on a sensational note, or touch:

> *What a thrill—*
> *My thumb instead of an onion.*
> *The top quite gone*
> *Except for a sort of hinge*
>
> *Of skin,*
> *A flap like a hat,*
> *Dead white.*
> *Then that red plush.*

This is vivid, no denying it. Morbid too. The question is whether the morbidity is an experience the writer struggles with or yields to, examines dispassionately or caresses indulgently.

There is a saving wit in the opening lines ('My thumb instead of an onion') and this provides some necessary distance between invoked experience and invoking speaker. But the poem collapses through Sylvia Plath's inability to do more with her theme than thrust it against our eyes, displaying her wound in all its red plushy woundedness.

> *The stain on your*
> *Gauze Ku Klux Klan*
> *Babushka*
> *Darkens and tarnishes . . .*

The bandage is seen as a babushka, an old lady's scarf. All right. But the Ku Klux Klan? And still more dubious, the 'Ku Klux Klan Babushka?' One supposes the KKK is being used here because it is whitely repressive, the Babushka-bandage is 're-pressing' the blood, and in the poem's graphic pathology, the flow of blood from the cut is attractive, fruitful, perhaps healthy ('a celebration, this is', runs one line). But even if my reading is accurate, does that help us very much with the stanza? Isn't it an example of weakness through excess?

Sylvia Plath's most famous poem, adored by many sons and daughters, is 'Daddy'. It is a poem with an affecting theme, the feelings of the speaker as she regathers the pain of her father's premature death and her persuasion that he has betrayed her by dying:

> *I was ten when they buried you.*
> *At twenty I tried to die*
> *And get back, back, back to you.*

In the poem Sylvia Plath identifies the father (we recall his German birth) with the Nazis ('Panzer-man, panzer-man, O You') and flares out with assaults for which nothing in the poem (nor, so far as we know, in Sylvia Plath's own life) offers any warrant: 'A cleft in your chin instead of your foot/

But no less a devil for that . . .' Nor does anything in the poem offer warrant, other than the free-flowing hysteria of the speaker, for the assault of such lines as, 'There's a stake in your fat black heart/ And the villagers never liked you.' Or for the snappy violence of

> *Every woman adores a Fascist,*
> *The boot in the face, the brute*
> *Brute heart of a brute like you.*

What we have here is a revenge fantasy, feeding upon filial love-hatred, and thereby mostly of clinical interest. But seemingly aware that the merely clinical can't provide the materials for a satisfying poem, Sylvia Plath tries to enlarge upon the personal plight, give meaning to the personal outcry, by fancying the girl as victim of a Nazi father:

> *An engine, an engine*
> *Chuffing me off like a Jew.*
> *A Jew to Dachau, Auschwitz, Belsen.*
> *I began to talk like a Jew,*
> *I think I may well be a Jew.*

The more sophisticated admirers of this poem may say that I fail to see it as a dramatic presentation, a monologue spoken by a disturbed girl not necessarily to be identified with Sylvia Plath, despite the similarities of detail between the events of the poem and the events of her life. I cannot accept this view. The personal-confessional element, strident and undisciplined, is simply too obtrusive to suppose the poem no more than a dramatic picture of a certain style of disturbance. If, however, we did accept such a reading of 'Daddy', we would fatally narrow its claims to emotional or moral significance, for we would be confining it to a mere vivid imagining of a pathological state. That, surely, is not how its admirers really take the poem.

It is clearly not how the critic George Steiner takes the poem when he calls it 'the "Guernica" of modern poetry'. But then, in an astonishing turn, he asks: 'In what sense does anyone, himself uninvolved and long after the event, commit a subtle larceny when he invokes the echoes and trappings of Auschwitz and appropriates an enormity of ready emotion to his own private design?' The question is devastating to his early comparison with 'Guernica'. Picasso's painting objectifies the horrors of Guernica, through the distancing of art; no one can suppose that he shares or participates in them. Plath's poem aggrandizes on the 'enormity of ready emotion' invoked by references to the concentration camps, in behalf of an ill-controlled if occasionally brilliant outburst. There is something monstrous, utterly disproportionate, when tangled emotions about one's father are deliberately compared with the historical fate of the European Jews; something sad, if the comparison is made spontaneously. 'Daddy' persuades one again, through the force of negative example, of how accurate T. S. Eliot was in saying, 'The more perfect the artist, the more completely separate in him will be the man who suffers and the mind which creates.'

III

The most interesting poems in *Ariel* are not confessional at all. A confessional poem would seem to be one in which the writer speaks *to* the reader, telling him, without the mediating presence of imagined event or *persona*, something about his life: I had a nervous breakdown, my wife and I sometimes lie in bed, sterile of heart, through sterile nights. The sense of direct speech addressed to an audience is central to confessional writing. But the most striking poems Sylvia Plath wrote are quite different. They are poems written out of an extreme condition, a state of being in which the speaker, for all practical purposes Sylvia Plath herself, has abandoned the sense of audience and cares nothing about – indeed, is hardly aware of – the presence of anyone but herself. She writes with a hallucinatory, self-contained fervor. She addresses herself to the air, to the walls. She speaks not as a daylight self, with its familiar internal struggles and doubts, its familiar hesitations before the needs and pressures of others. There is something utterly monolithic, fixated about the voice that emerges in these poems, a voice unmodulated and asocial.

It's as if we are overhearing the rasps of a mind that has found its own habitation and need not measure its distance from, even consider its relation to, other minds. And the stakes are far higher than can ever be involved in mere confession. She exists in some mediate province between living and dying, and she appears to be balancing coolly the claims of the two, drawn almost equally to both yet oddly comfortable with the perils of where she is. This is not the by-now worn romanticism of *Liebestod*. It is something very strange, very fearful: a different kind of existence, at ease at the gate of dying. The poems Sylvia Plath wrote in this state of being are not 'great' poems, but one can hardly doubt that they are remarkable. For they do bring into poetry an element of experience that, so far as I know, is new, and thereby they advance the thrust of literary modernism by another inch or so. A poem like 'Kindness' is set squarely in what I have called the mediate province between living and dying:

> *What is so real as the cry of a child?*
> *A rabbit's cry may be wilder*
> *But it has no soul.*

And then, a few lines later:

> *The blood jet is poetry,*
> *There is no stopping it.*

The poems written out of this strange equilibrium – 'Fever 103', 'Totem', 'Edge' – are notable, and the best of them seems to me 'Edge':

The woman is perfected.
Her dead

Body wears the smile of accomplishment,
The illusion of a Greek necessity

Flows in the scrolls of her toga,
Her bare

Feet seem to be saying:
We have come so far, it is over.

Each dead child coiled, a white serpent,
One at each little

Pitcher of milk, now empty.
She has folded

Them back into her body as petals
Of a rose close when the garden

Stiffens and odours bleed
From the sweet, deep throats of the night flower.

The moon has nothing to be sad about,
Staring from her hood of bone.

She is used to this sort of thing.
Her blacks crackle and drag.

The vision of death as composure, a work done well, is beautifully realized in the first four stanzas. The next several, with 'Each dead child coiled, a white serpent', seem to me to drop into a kind of sensationalism – not the kind one finds in the confessional poems, with their alternating archness and violence, but one that invokes the completion that may come once death is done and finished. The penultimate stanza is very fine; the last lines again seem forced.

Even in this kind of poetry, which does strike an original note, there are many limitations. The poems often shock; they seldom surprise. They are deficient in plasticity of feeling, the modulation of voice that a poet writing out of a controlled maturity of consciousness can muster. Even the best of Sylvia Plath's poems, as her admirer Stephen Spender admits, 'have little principle of beginning or ending, but seem fragments, not so much of one long poem, as of an outpouring which could not stop with the lapsing of the poet's hysteria.'

Perhaps the hardest critical question remains. Given the fact that in a few poems Sylvia Plath illustrates an extreme state of existence, one at the very boundary of nonexistence, what illumination – moral, psychological, social – can be provided of either this state or the general human condition by a writer so deeply rooted in the extremity of her plight? Suicide is an eternal possibility of our life and therefore always interesting; but what is the relation between a sensibility so deeply captive to the idea of suicide and the claims and possibilities of human existence in general? That her story is intensely moving, that her talent was notable, that her final breakthrough rouses admiration – of course! Yet in none of the essays devoted to praising Sylvia Plath have I found a coherent statement as to the nature, let alone the value, of her vision. Perhaps it is assumed that to enter the state of mind in which she found herself at the end of her life is its own ground for high valuation; but what will her admirers say to those who reply that precisely this assumption is what needs to be questioned?

56

After the noise abates and judgment returns, Sylvia Plath will be regarded as an interesting minor poet whose personal story was poignant. A few of her poems will find a place in anthologies – and when you consider the common fate of talent, that, after all, will not be a small acknowledgment.

The Critical Point
Horizon Press

Poems from Books

Fleur Adcock **In Memoriam: James K. Baxter**

Dear Jim, I'm using a Shakespearian form
to write you what I'll call a farewell letter.
Rhyming iambics have become the norm
for verse epistles, and I'm no trendsetter.
Perhaps you'll think it's going back a bit,
but as a craftsman you'll approve of it.

What better model have we, after all?
Dylan the Welshman, long your youthful passion,
doesn't quite do now, and the dying fall
of Eliot was never in your fashion.
Of North Americans the one you'd favour
is Lowell. But his salt has the wrong savour:

our ocean's called Pacific, not Atlantic –
which doesn't mean to say Neruda meets
the case. As for the classically romantic –
well, maybe it was easier for Keats:
I'd write with more conviction about death
if it were clutching at my every breath.

And now we've come to it. The subject's out:
the ineluctable, the all-pervasive.
Your death is what this letter's all about;
and if so far I've seemed a bit evasive
it's not from cowardice or phoney tact –
it's simply that I can't believe the fact.

I'd put you, with New Zealand, in cold storage
to wait for my return (should I so choose).
News of destruction can't delete an image:
what isn't seen to go, one doesn't lose.
The bulldozed streets, the buildings they've torn
   down
remain untouched until I'm back in town.

And so with you, framed in that sepia vision
a hemisphere away from me, and half

the twenty years I've known you. Such division
converts a face into a photograph:
a little blurred perhaps, the outlines dim,
but fixed, enduring, permanently Jim.

I saw you first when I was seventeen,
a word-struck student, ripe for dazzling. You
held unassuming court in the canteen –
the famous poet in the coffee-queue.
I watched with awe. But soon, as spheres are apt
to do in Wellington, ours overlapped.

I married, you might say, into the art.
You were my husband's friend; you'd wander in
on your way home from teaching, at the start,
for literary shop-talk over gin.
And then those fabled parties of one's youth:
home-brew and hot-lines to poetic truth.

Later the drinks were tea and lemonade,
the visits family ones, the talk less vatic;
and later still, down south, after I'd made
my getaway, came idiosyncratic
letters, your generous comments on my verse,
and poems of your own. But why rehearse

matters which you, acute observer, wise
recorder, don't forget? And now I falter,
knowing your present case: those tolerant eyes
will register no more. But I can't alter
this message to a dirge; the public attitude
isn't my style: I write in simple gratitude.

To think of elegies is to recall
several of yours. I find, when I look through
your varied, eloquent poems, nearly all
frosted with hints at death. What can I do
now, when it has become your own condition,
but praise all that you gave to the tradition?

The Scenic Route, Oxford University Press

John Betjeman   **Back from Australia**

Cocooned in Time, at this inhuman height,
  The packaged food tastes neutrally of clay.
  We never seem to catch the running day
But travel on in everlasting night
With all the chic accoutrements of flight:
  Lotions and essences in neat array
  And yet another plastic cup and tray.
'Thank you *so* much. Oh no, I'm quite all right'.

At home in Cornwall hurrying autumn skies
  Leave Bray Hill barren, Stepper jutting bare,
    And hold the moon above the sea-wet sand.
The very last of late September dies
  In frosty silence and the hills declare
    How vast the sky is, looked at from the land.

A Nip in the Air, John Murray

1

I named it sickle. But he
uses it, the old man, and he called it:
the hook.

No longer new; a flatter curve
of blade than the gold on red: crescent
of an ellipse;

and implement, not emblem:
dull, rust oiled with usage; nicked, the
harshened silver edge.

But a tool perfects, almost
like nature; more stringent than art, millenia
winnowed to this

shape since Egypt was
the world's grainhouse, longer:
a moon-edge

cutting finer than the straight:
grass, not flesh: only the point would embed,
opening an enemy

like a full sack, or the edge
hack a limb, the swung fist past its mark;
but savage enough

a symbol of agronomy
for rising serfs. The crossed hammer beat
this out blue once

in a man's fist; but mass
produced now for a dwindling few, this tool,
this weapon:

the steel flattened, arched, made
keen, even the white ash turned smooth, and
ferruled, by machine.

But finely weighted, this one:
light, as if I held only a handle, even
to the left hand,

even as it learns the backsweep.
I stooped and swung; the wristy, ambidextral hook
slew grass,

forestroke and back. I think
no eye but wrist bought this; by balanced weight,
like grain;

and that it is beautiful only
now, for the coarse use that refined it,
like the sea-stone.

2
Beautiful too is the word:
swathe. I laid low all afternoon tall, green,
slender seeded grasses

of more elegance than poplars.
Their stems fell sheaved after the stroke
like armfuls of bluebells;

the blade was wet with sap.
Doubled I stooped, and climbed the field
all the hot afternoon

for these red stigmata,
skinned blisters on the mounts of
both white palms.

3 Young Anglo Welsh Poets, Welsh Arts Council

Iain Crichton Smith   **The Sound of Music**

After the *Sound of Music* we mooned out
into the street again. Glasgow by night.
The pavement and the road were blue and wet.
There wasn't a single rainy close without
a couple kissing. They wore narrow tights
and clung together in the plaguey lights
infecting their white faces. It was not
what one would call a fine attractive sight.
It was a whimpering wolfish appetite.

It wasn't really like the *Sound of Music*
with all those Viennese waltzes and the like,
the roomy castles, staircases, the stock
of trilling nuns more musical than Catholic,
their sudden warbles, eloquent technique,
but everyone so cheery and so slick.
They seemed to sing whenever they should speak
and all so nice and pricey as in *Vogue*.

Through the blue and green of Glasgow we strolled
         on
by Indian restaurants and Chinese ones.
Cropped youths stalked past us in their mottled
         skin,
their glinting eyes expressionless as stone.
There was a dance hall coloured violent green
and slogans six foot high made yellow stains
on rotting tenements. I could see no nuns
and nowhere marbled halls or chanting children
but swaying drunks so miserably alone

that convents could not reach them, nor God's ways
which chimed with Hollywood's refined arias
that even the gauleiters could not suppress.
The screen, uncracked by bottle or by vice,
reflected perfect flawless families.

I did not walk in fear but saw each dress
as in a radiance which I must prize
not freshly laundered nor as Viennese
but stained with sweat to a more tense repose.

The Notebooks of Robinson Crusoe, Gollancz

Iain Crichton Smith   **Journey**

At nighttime we drive home under the trees.
The rabbits bolt before us, and the hares,
and an owl wafts slowly past. The light is green
and then you say, 'Suppose when we draw in,
to the town, I mean, the small town that is ours,
there's no one there, they've vanished . . .' And I
        said,
jokingly without thinking, 'Well, I'd raid
the houses for their jewellery and TV,
their radios and purses.'
                A moon shed
its light around us on the autumn corn.
It blazed in the bluish sky, a full round moon
And then I thought, 'Suppose it were really true.'
I stare at the green light and then at you
and think of the two of us set quite alone
in the small town we know and shivering say,
'That was a joke of course.' And then you say,
'Mine was a joke as well.' But did you see
the ghosts I saw hitchhiking by the road
with their foggy packs where not even weasels go
and did you think the thought I suddenly thought
of the white lines that never end but flow
through towns that once were there but now are
        not?

The Notebooks of Robinson Crusoe, Gollancz

Donald Davie   **Westmorland**

Kendal . . . Shap Fell! Is that in Westmorland?
For one who espouses the North,
I am hazy about it, frankly. It's a chosen
North of the mind I take my bearings by,
A stripped style and a wintry;

As on Shap Fell, the only time I was there,
Wind cutting over and snowflakes beginning to sail
Slantwise across, on haulage vans clashing their
    gears
And me who had walked from Glasgow.

An end-of-October taste, a shade too late
For the right full ripeness. The style is decadent
    almost,
Emaciated, flayed. One knows such shapes,
Such minds, such people, always in need of a touch
Of frost, not to go pulpy.

The Shires, Routledge

When I was ten, going to Hamilton
On the Leyland bus named for Eddlewood,
A boy with an aeroplane just like mine
Zoomed at his war games in the seat in front.
I'd never seen such a school uniform –
As brown as the manure in Cousar's coup
Where someone's city cousin had jumped in
Having been told it was 'just sand' –
One of Glasgow's best fee-paying places,
Brown as barrowloads from the blue-bottled byre.
I couldn't help it; I had to talk to him
And tell him I, too, had a Hurricane.
His mother pulled him to her, he sat sullen,
As if I'd spoiled his game. I spoke again,
And he called me a poor boy, who should shut up.
I'd never thought of it like that.
The summer tenements were so dry I cried.
My grandfather wouldn't give *him* sixpence;
He'd never have a grudge as lovely as mine.

Years later, running in a race, barefooted
As I'd trained my spikes to ruin, convinced
My best competitor was him, I ran into
The worse weathers of pain, determined to win,
But on the last lap, inches from the tape, was beaten
By someone from Shotts Miners' Welfare Harriers
    Club.

Love or Nothing, Faber

Douglas Dunn   **I Am a Cameraman**

They suffer, and I catch only the surface.
The rest is inexpressible, beyond
What can be recorded. You can't be them.
If they'd talk to you, you might guess
What pain is like though they might spit on you.

Film is just a reflection
Of the matchless despair of the century.
There have been twenty centuries since charity
        began.
Indignation is day-to-day stuff;
It keeps us off the streets, it keeps us watching.

Film has no words of its own.
It is a silent waste of things happening
Without us, when it is too late to help.
What of the dignity of those caught suffering?
It hurts me. I robbed them of privacy.

My young friends think Film will be all of Art.
It will be revolutionary proof.
Their films will not guess wrongly and will not lie.
They'll film what is happening behind barbed wire.
They'll always know the truth and be famous.

Politics softens everything.
Truth is known only to its victims.
All else is photographs – a documentary
The starving and the playboys perish in.
Life disguises itself with professionalism.

Life tells the biggest lies of all,
And draws wages from itself.
Truth is a landscape the saintly tribes live on,
And all the lenses of Japan and Germany
Wouldn't know how to focus on it.

Life flickers on the frame like beautiful
    hummingbirds.
That is the film that always comes out blank.
The painting the artist can't get shapes to fit.
The poem that shrugs off every word you try.
The music no one has ever heard.

Love or Nothing, Faber

Bryn Griffiths   Dolphins

The shimmering sea is still –
till a detonation in the deeps
sends the gentle fury exploding

upwards, upwards, towards the bright
roof of the world where the dark
green of the world

pales into another sea
of incredible light:
the sky breaks, shatters, parts

under the soaring hurl of silver
weight that splits the waterface
with white spray:

a school of dolphin flashes
into sight . . . And here we watch,
we shackled men,

while the dolphins wheel and spin
and march in foaming echelons
through the long hot day to weigh

our minds with millenial doubt
of man's ways – the lack of fluke
and fin to surge deep and swim.

Our ship drives on, a dust mote
on the waterclock, and now
the day dies to bring down night

in the swift tropic extinction
of light as the dolphins drift away,
leaving two alone to watch over us,

knifing through the night alongside,
scissoring endlessly, leap over leap,
in the green fire of phosphorescence

which breaks about our bow . . .
For miles, long sea miles, they hurtle
alongside, their fixed grin of ages

seeming to pity us, and then
they wheel away in sudden flight –
their bulleting bodies gone into night!

The Dark Convoys, Aquila

Geoffrey Grigson   **Young and Old**

You are young, you two, in loving:
Why should you wonder what endearments
Old whisper still to old in bed,
Or what the one left will say and say,
Aloud, when nobody overhears, to the one
who irremediably is dead?

Angles and Circles, Gollancz

Geoffrey Grigson   **One Surface of Loving**

How is it I have not celebrated
Your under-arm, from your wrist
To your elbow?

It is one of your
Gentlest surfaces, and at this moment
It lies on my cheek.

I have only to turn my head
Very slightly and my lips are
Against this surface of loving,

But you remove your arm from me
And instead you are now
Stroking my head.

Angles and Circles, Gollancz

James Hamilton
Paterson

latin lesson

of course it's not
dead they said
because you start right in
with thrills: practically learn
to run before you walk.
ignore but memorise

the first word
amo i love.
altogether now
i thou he-she-or-it
we you (pl.) they.
amant: everybody's doing it

but not for long.
from dusty scabbards
flash real weapons
across the pages
flee slaves and enemies
dying in every tense.

even at the end
citadels still fall
and generals
command the last attack
but more long-windedly
and sometimes conditionally.

they wield death
in sentences
by with or from a horse
often in a camp.
balbus slept here
is not scratched

on a wall and
caesar is not mentioned
in despatches as
small bald and queer.
only the stark downpour
of darts and the terror of horses

and the barbarians who were
or were not
about to be or thought
to be about to be
killing MDCCC prisoners or
hostages ad lib.

simpler to ride
with caesar and his soldier's
plain language:
to follow brilliant campaigns
than parse tricky things
by catullus

poems about kisses.
hard to believe that any
red blooded boy would rather
wander with lesbia through
lemon groves than
run with cohorts

Option Three, Gollancz

James Hamilton-
Paterson

From **Option Three**

Which was how they found him,
beached on one elbow,
hair flat and mouth
plugged with shingle, nothing
but horizons all
around and the sea
smooth as cropped turf.
He opened colourless eyes
which were to have been
pressed by infinite salt,
saw only the silent
ring of those who stood.
From his hanging mouth
stones fell and shells
and threads of seaweed. It
was all he had to say.
His antrums, sinuses
and ears full, his head
rang like a flask.
Faintly their whispers blew
past him. One of them said:
There are no accidents,
and he acknowledged it was
true as anything he had
found caught in the hinges
of the sea.
                    When
they left, their feet had made
no pattern of the scuffed
sand but he could see,
through mucus, not
a grain was out of place.
Time passed and the gulls
left him as the light
dimmed and even the crabs

mustered unseen their brittle
army to peel his face.
But they came out with the stars,
and carefully the moon
drew water over his head.

Option Three, Gollancz

John Hewitt   **The Search**
for Shirley and Darryl

We left the western island to live among strangers
in a city older by centuries
than the market town which we had come from
where the slow river spills out between green hills
and gulls perch on the bannered poles.

It is a hard responsibility to be a stranger;
to hear your speech sounding at odds with your
        neighbours;
holding your tongue from quick comparisons;
remembering that you are a guest in the house.

Often you will regret the voyage,
wakening in the dark night to recall that other place
or glimpsing the moon rising and recollecting
that it is also rising over named hills,
shining on known waters.

But sometimes the thought
that you have not come away from, but returned,
to this older place whose landmarks are yours also,
occurs when you look down a long street remarking
the architectural styles or move through a landscape
with wheat ripening in large fields.

Yet you may not rest here, having come back,
for this is not your abiding place, either.

The authorities declare that in former days
the western island was uninhabited,
just as where you reside now was once tundra,
and what you seek maybe no more than
a broken circle of stones on a rough hillside,
        somewhere.

Out of My Time, Blackstaff Press (Belfast)

Geoffrey Holloway   **Rhine Jump, 1944**

They dropped us on the guns, left us in a flaring
lurch of slipstream kicking like sprayed flies, –
till canopies shook sudden heads, inhaled, held a
    breath, –
alive again we slanted down,
too many, into their doomed sights.

One scrambled moment it was red, green,
dragging to the door of the Douglas then
falling through a monstrous aviary roof
on Guy Fawkes Night (only this was day)
into shrill scarifying glory . . .

then Germany, the Fatherland, a zooming field –
banged down on it, stood up among the chaos, with
fingers flopped like rubber gloves trying
to slap one's box, slough the afterbirth of chute,
make somehow that snatch of wood.

There were chutes already in those trees, caught:
battalion boys who'd dropped too late or drifted . . .
harness-ravelled, cocooned there –
like silkworms, moveless, wet . . .
so easy, against all that white.

But not so many resistive earthworms –
the early birds had seen to that.
Soon, it was rendezvous: a stodgy farm.
The war was folding: fight-thin.
Prisoners happened; columned, toneless.

Next day it was hearing tales again,
having a kip in a pigsty, scouting the dropping-zone
to get silk (knickers for sweethearts, wives);
maybe a green envelope, speculation
about leave, Japan.

Oh and a gun-pit by the way, an 88,
bodiless, nothing special,
only the pro's interest in other's kit:
grey slacks for the use of, old, ersatz;
with a brown inside stripe: non-ersatz.

Rhine Jump, London Magazine Editions

Counting back from the crossing-gates –
thirteen people taking about a hundred
yards. All engines off: pathetic but diligent
ecologists who can do no more.
After the train had smacked through at ninety
dead empty with all lights blazing
and the keeper like an old-fashioned man
with a pride in his work had scampered
down steps and let us through full pelt
it was clear one woman would not get started
not in our time there. Assuming
an engine stalled or something broken
we indicated, pulled out, passed her.
Only later, recalling
the small hand like a white rag
up at the mouth and the eyes riveted ahead
did it occur to me as it obviously occurred
to others judging by the fluttering brakelights
that not the car had broken, but the woman.

For Mad Mary, London Magazine Editions

Welcome aboard, says Wilson. We grip
Their smooth fingers in ours gnarled.
One moment after losing friends, off balance,
We stagger toward friendship
By dispensation of the Board, by chance.

One scratches at his nose, and smiles;
One clasps a book. Edging into a corner,
One settles in your chair. There's a climacteric
In our body, replacement of cells.
We might reverse it if we knew the trick

Or cared enough. *Mr Watson has been here
For two years. We give him* . . . the small token . . .
Silver, transmuted into dull pewter,
Today's pint tankard for tomorrow's small beer.
Applause. Speech. Speech. Tranquillity will neuter

And fade Jim Watson like a photograph
Who, pleasantly drunk and American, calls *Don't
    forget
Now, Don't forget boys:* Jim, we clap your back,
You fall into a taxi. Wave and laugh –
Wave through that darkened screen; we are losing
    track

Of you already. And these new men climb
Into your place as if into your clothes.
You are nowhere, unless somebody recalls
Those quips, the table roaring. *See you, Jim:*
We saw the last of you, in these arrivals.

Bicycle Tyre in a Tall Tree, Carcanet

Groping back to bed after a piss
I part thick curtains, and am startled by
The rapid clouds, the moon's cleanliness.

Four o'clock: wedge-shadowed garden lie
Under a cavernous, a wind-picked sky.
There's something laughable about this,

The way the moon dashes through clouds that blow
Loosely as cannon-smoke to stand apart
(Stone-coloured light sharpening the roofs below)

High and preposterous and separate –
Lozenge of love! Medallion of art!
O wolves of memory! Immensements! No,

One shivers slightly, looking up there.
The hardness and the brightness and the plain
Far-reaching singleness of that wide stare

Is a reminder of the strength and pain
Of being young; that it can't come again,
But is for others undiminished somewhere.

High Windows, Faber

Philip Larkin   **High Windows**

When I see a couple of kids
And guess he's fucking her and she's
Taking pills or wearing a diaphragm,
I know this is paradise

Everyone old has dreamed of all their lives –
Bonds and gestures pushed to one side
Like an outdated combine harvester,
And everyone young going down the long slide

To happiness, endlessly. I wonder if
Anyone looked at me, forty years back,
And thought, *That'll be the life;*
No God any more, or sweating in the dark

About hell and that, or having to hide
What you think of the priest. He
And his lot will all go down the long slide
Like free bloody birds. And immediately

Rather than words comes the thought of high
    windows:
The sun-comprehending glass,
And beyond it, the deep blue air, that shows
Nothing, and is nowhere, and is endless.

High Windows, Faber

Alan Sillitoe   **Lamppost**

Strong, once permanent, and twelve feet tall,
An obsolescent lamp post
Is about to be uprooted
By a block-and-tackle gibbet,
One of many planted on that street –
Whose incandescent memories
Are cool and out for good.

Fluted trunk and crosstrees high
Head uplifted and extinguished:
Once its sober glare lit tracks
For boozers weaving late from pubs:
A beanpole for mad cars to bump at –
A man once tried to stare it out:
Gas fed its flame. God turned it off.

A question-hook spins up
(Unfitted for the lamp post's view)
By a workman in his cabin
Sorting levers like a hangman,
Who holds the still full-vigoured beacon
Lopsided for a final look along the street:

Crashes out of sunlight, into lorry.

Storm, W. H. Allen

Christ is the language which we speak to God
And also God, so that we speak in truth;
He in us, we in him, speaking
To one another, to Him, the City of God.

I.

Such a fool as I am you had better ignore
Tongue twist, malevolent, fat mouthed
I have no language but that other one
His the Devil's, no mouse I, creeping out of the
    cheese
With a peaked cap scanning the distance
Looking for truth.
Words when I have them, come out, the Devil
Encouraging, grinning from the other side of the
    street
And my tears
Streaming, a blubbered face, when I am not laughing
Where in all this
Is calm, measure,
Exactness
The Lord's peace?

II.

Nothing is in my own voice because I have not
Any. Nothing in my own name
Here inscribed on water, nothing but flow
A ripple, outwards. Standing beside the Usk
You flow like truth, river, I will get in
Over me, through me perhaps, river let me be
    crystalline
As I shall not be, shivering upon the bank.
A swan passed. So is it, the surface, sometimes
Benign like a mirror, but not I passing, the bird.

III.

Under the bridge, meet reward, the water
Falling in cascades or worse, you devil, for
  truthfulness
Is no part of the illusion, the clear sky
Is not yours, the water
Falling not yours
Only the sheep
Munching at the river brim
Perhaps

IV.

What I had hoped for, the clear line
Tremulous like water but
Clear also to the stones underneath
Has not come that way, for my truth
Was not public enough, not perhaps true.
Holy Father, Almighty God
Stop me before I speak

— *per Christum.*

V.

Lies on my tongue. Get up and bolt the door
For I am coming not to be believed
The messenger of anything I say.
So I am come, stand in the cold tonight
The servant of the grain upon my tongue,
Beware, I am the man, and let me in.

VI.

So speech is treasured, for the things it gives
Which I can not have, for I speak too plain
Yet not so plain as to be understood
It is confusion and a madman's tongue.
Where drops the reason, there is no one by.
Torture my mind: and so swim through the night
As envy cannot touch you, or myself
Sleep comes, and let her, warm at my side, like
  death,

The Holy Spirit and the Holy One
Of Israel be my guide. So among tombs
Truth may be sought, and found, if we rejoice
With Ham and Shem and Japhet in the dark
The ark rolls onward over a wide sea.
Come sleep, come lightening, comes the dove at last.

In a Trojan Ditch, Carcanet

A *Saint*, they said, *A Saint*!
And there she lay,
naked, entranced in her cell.
I wove my web
between the stiff rapt thighs.
They held their breaths
in awe to see
the cunning of the veil

I spun from the hate in my gut
on that spotless place,
for I am the Lady of Traps –
my every lover's
post-coital sadness
meets my bite;
I hoe their legs at the joints;
I crush up armour.

Yet she lay easy,
breathing but unmoving,
trapped by her soul into stillness.
I ate flies
between the lips of her vulva.
She never stirred
but the once to whisper *Beloved*. . . .
Was I the adored?

I, the Lady of Silence?
I choke mouths,
blind eyeballs, shroud the tombs.
I am the dream
that drifts through palpitations.
I slide my net
across the coupling buttocks
of Mars and Venus,

the agent of shame and wisdom.
I crouch at the centre
garnering paralysis, waiting. . . .
Could I be dear
to any trapped or victim?
Who is the victim?
The buzzing of prayers has ended.
I scuttle to supper.

Timelight, Heinemann

Reading you the story you cannot understand
any more than another, before the light
goes out, I am distracted by the hand
turning the page too early or too late –

as I was in the bookshop, hearing today
that other father with the small son say:
'We need a book. What would you recommend
for a four-year-old starting to read?'

And a dam in my head broke under the thought
of things your simple hand would never make:
toys, love, and poems scattering the comfort
of commandments you can never break.

Hand in Hand, Chatto and The Hogarth Press

This milky sky of a dragging afternoon
  Seems a painter's sky – the vision of a lack,
A thwarted possibility that broods
  On the meanness and exclusion. This could well be
An afternoon sunk in eternity
  But for the traffic tolling the rush hour
Among blackened houses, back to back
  And the tang of the air (its milk is sour:)
And what painting could taste of such dragging
    afternoons
  Whose tints are tainted, whose Fujiyamas slag?

The Way In, Oxford University Press

Charles Tomlinson   **Dates: Penkhull New Road**

It was new about eighteen-sixty.
Eighteen-sixty had come to stay, and did
Until the war – the second war, I mean.
Wasn't forty-five our nineteen-seventeen –
The revolution we had all of us earned?
Streamers and trestles in the roadway:
Even the climate rhymed with the occasion
And no drop fell. Eighteen-sixty
The architecture still insisted, gravely neat:
Alleyways between the houses, doors
That opened onto a still car-less street.
Doorsteps were once a civil place. There must have
    been a date
It came to be thought common and too late
In time, to be standing shouting out there
Across to the other side – the side
I envied, because its back-yards ran sheer
To the factory wall, warm, black, pulsating,
A long, comforting brick beast. I returned
In seventy-three. Like England,
The place had half-moved with the times – the
    'other side'
Was gone. Something had bitten a gap
Out of the stretch we lived in. Penkhull still crowned
The hill, rebuilt to a plan – may as well scrap
The architectural calendar: that dream
Was dreamed up by the insurance-man
And we've a long time to live it yet.
The factory wore a half-bereaved, half-naked
    look . . .
It took time to convince me that I cared
For more than beauty: I write to rescue
What is no longer there – absurd
A place should be more fragile than a book.

The Way In, Oxford University Press.

I should be grateful. You
adopted me in a hard time,
the sound of guns from Dunkirk shaking
London, the bombs. You have told
how once you lay over my pram as a German
aeroplane swooped to machine-gun the street.
What made you, you never did say.

It was only 'You should be grateful' became
the theme you played on a subtle keyboard
(you'd not been an actress in vain):
grateful for supper, for half-days in Brighton,
for wellington boots in rainy weather,
'For all I have done for you.'
There was also your tone saying 'Don't.'

And when father left you said nothing,
except – remember? – when
I finally asked, that day in the park
at the rusted green cafeteria seats,
to distract me, 'Look at those sparrows,'
and did not notice rage boiling the dregs
of a nine-year-old's childhood away.

So I locked you from me in turn, as I locked
my schoolwork away in a case.
Where was I going? 'Out.'
And when leaving for good I came
to tell you, you carried on hanging up washing,
not taking the peg from your mouth just said
'Remember to leave your doorkey.'

At seventy now, arthritis
has withered the touch and range
from your piano-player's hands,
your first teeth are gone (years after mine).
Hoarding a fossil faith
in Stalin, the god that failed,
you keep up the garden, read Dickens, see plays,

and we can be easier together,
and I am truly grateful.
If what you pinched and scraped once seemed
me, I know now it was for me,
understand things you still cannot say
as your talkative letters come, each signed
not 'with love', just 'as ever'.

Living Room, The Marvell Press

Andrew Waterman   **A Butterfly**

Even under the shed there's something outdoors
about the work. One side stands open

to stars and wind. You pause on your barrow to
    watch
dawn come up, or a shower across the city.

You're never bricked in. On slack shifts in summer
men wander off along overgrown sidings,
    embankments,

for a sun and a glance through the *Mirror*: a couple
have planted a vegetable-garden back of
    Humberstone Coal Wharf.

96

Grass invades. Dustiest corners are settled
with unauthorised flowers. The Grain Shed sparrows

strut plundering leaking sacks, great rats
buck-jump away from right under your feet.

On a fine day wagons trundle in hung with glittering
waterdrops: somewhere rain is falling.

Even one bleak night, surrounded
by foggy blackness, and cartons, crates,

rolls of netting stacked up on the shed-platform,
hard graft, something broke in when old Gumble
    found

in the straw that wadded a cased-up carboy of acid
a sleepy butterfly. It crawled

on to his palm. 'Beautiful little bugger,
in't it?' It fluttered in his sour beer breath.

'Look at this, Jacko. Red Admiral.' Wherever
he carried it, cupped precious in his hands,

men stopped, gathering under wan lights:
blue overalls, stubbled faces focused on

a butterfly, straw strewn upon the concrete,
and birds starting racketing for the new day in the
    girders.

Living Room, The Marvell Press

Points of View

> *White-shield* Worthington *was still*
> *Around and we'd got time to kill*
> *(Pages were harder than beer-mugs to fill.)*
> *We broke the tape*
> *Playing bar-billiards until*
> *The thing took shape.*

Thus John Fuller, in January 1973, recalling how perhaps ten years earlier he and Ian Hamilton, with presumably one or two others, prepared themselves for the assault on literary England that was subsequently carried through in the pages of Hamilton's magazine *The Review*. Ten or twelve or perhaps fifteen years before, those same Oxford pubs where Fuller and Hamilton drank Worthington, had seen John Wain and Kingsley Amis, with presumably one or two others (Wallace Robson? Arthur Boyars? sometimes Philip Larkin?), preparing for the assault that, by way of Wain's radio programme *New Soundings*, established itself as 'the Movement', recorded in Robert Conquest's anthology *New Lines* and George Hartley's magazine *Listen*. Ten or so years before that the plotters in the pubs were Sidney Keyes and Drummond Allison; ten years earlier still, they were Wystan Auden and Stephen Spender; and ten or so years after John Fuller and Ian Hamilton they were, I suppose, Michael Schmidt and Grevel Lindop and Gareth Reeves.

I may be wrong about some of the details, for I was not present on any of these occasions. But the general picture is surely accurate; for the last fifty years each new generation of English poets, as the 'generations' were subsequently to be understood and talked about by journalistic commentators, was formed or fomented or dreamed up by lively undergraduates at Oxford, who subsequently carried the group-image to London and from there imposed it on the public consciousness so as to earn at least a footnote in the literary histories.

Earlier than any of these, and a more massively successful take-over bid than any of them, had been one that originated not in Oxford but Cambridge – the famous and all too abundantly documented Bloomsbury Group. This assault however had been on an altogether wider front, and was not exclusively nor even mainly a literary movement; in particular it lost its predestined poet when Rupert Brooke died in 1915, and subsequently the best it could do was to co-opt, never very securely, the Oxonian American T. S. Eliot. At any rate, ever since that Cambridge take-over in the 1920s, every new *putsch* has come from Oxford and has picked up its Cambridge recruits (Christopher Isherwood in one generation, Thom Gunn in another) only afterwards, and incidentally.

But (it may be said) are there no universities and university-towns in England apart from these two? There are; *Poetry Nation* is edited from one of them, as *Critical Quarterly* is from another, as Jon Silkin's *Stand* from another. And the literary life of England would be in a healthier state if we had to allow for the possibility that at this moment two or three literary-minded students in Manchester, two or three more in Newcastle, two or three more in the University of East Anglia, were planning a take-over of literary London such as has been planned in Oxford time and again, and carried through from there successfully. But there is no recorded instance of such a *putsch* from any redbrick university, nor any reason to think that things have changed so as to make one likely; and as for the new universities of the 1960s, some of us who were involved in setting them up dared to hope that indeed they might break the Oxbridge stranglehold on our literary life – a hope very quickly dashed as one after another of them showed that their interests lay quite elsewhere, in the sub-politics of self-righteous confrontation.

However that may be, and wherever the assault may be planned, the objective has to be London. William Webb has for many years worked wonders with the Book Page of the *Guardian*, as a literary forum, which, though edited from the provinces, is not provincial in taste. But that is the only weekly or even monthly publication of which one can say as much; every other publication in which a literary reputation can be made or unmade emanates from London. And we all know which these influential organs are – the merest handful: *The Times Literary Supplement*, the *New Statesman*, the *Listener*, the *London Magazine*, the *Observer*; together with, much more dubiously, the *Spectator*, *Encounter*, the *Sunday Times*. Precisely because the positions that matter are so few, it is entirely feasible for a group to secure one or two sub-editorial chairs and a few reviewing 'spots', so as to impose their shared proclivities and opinions as the reigning orthodoxy for a decade. It is altogether fatuous to cry out at this as scandalous; it is inevitable, given the smallness of England, and the economic advantages of metropolitan centralisation. Quite simply, these are the facts that have to be borne in mind by any one who, like Ian Hamilton ten or twelve years ago, wants to affect the level or the direction of the nation's literary taste. From a careerist's point of view the magazine by which the group identifies itself before the public – in Hamilton's case, *The Review* – is only a means to an end; in its pages, as in the debating-chamber of the Oxford or the Cambridge Union, the young critics put on their sparkling performances so as to be noticed by those who dispense the metropolitan plums. How successful Ian Hamilton was can be seen by checking how many of the names that now turn up regularly in the journals listed above, first appeared in the pages of *The Review*.

John Fuller, in his gay and engaging poem, 'To Ian Hamilton', made no bones about the fact that he was celebrating a success-story:

The Fat Men quivered at your glance,
Careers destroyed by your advance.
Still you are wooed at every chance
Like an heiress . . .

And indeed Fuller's 144 lines of skilful light verse were themselves part of a ceremonial triumph. For his poem, when published in the *Listener* for 25 January last, was followed by a review of the tenth anniversary issue of *The Review*, and of fifteen 'essays and reviews' by Ian Hamilton assembled into a slim volume under the title, *A Poetry Chronicle*; and the whole act of homage was high lighted on the cover of that issue of the *Listener* under the rubric, 'The Critic as Hero'. Nor was the *Listener* alone. A ground-swell of enthusiastic applause for *The Review*, and for Hamilton as its guiding intelligence, had been gathering for several years; and indeed for that very tenth anniversary issue of *The Review*, the editor had issued a questionnaire asking poets and pundits to identify hopeful developments in English poetry through the 1960s, thus inviting flattering tributes which came gratifyingly to hand. A success-story indeed! No critic's first book of criticism (or rather, more strikingly and more precisely, no reviewer's first assemblage of reprinted reviews) could have been received with more respect and attention than Hamilton's *A Poetry Chronicle*.

Good luck to him, therefore! Such success is not achieved without skill and patience (nor, I'm glad to say, without talent – but we'll come to that). In particular, even when the competition in any generation is by curious tacit consent limited to the University of Oxford, there is sure to be competition: two or three other young men, in the same Oxford pubs at different times, are sure to be hatching their plans even as you and your chums hatch yours. In Hamilton's case the competitors were William Cookson and Peter Dale (with a few others no doubt) who were hatching their *Agenda* before ever Hamilton and John Fuller and their friends, having tried and failed with a magazine called *Tomorrow*, began to work out the shape of *The Review*. Though Cookson was never (as it turned out) in the race for the metropolitan plums, his *Agenda* remains, for *The Review*, its worrying rival; as it was, John Fuller informs us, from the first:

> At least ten years ago there were no
> Worse than those who, sipping Pernod,
> In Lallans ruined the Inferno
> With tips from Pound.

Like many other of Fuller's sprightly stanzas, this one is written in a sort of code; but one does not have to be much of an initiate to decode this one. *Agenda*, defiantly and indeed with wearisome predictability devoted to the programmes of Ezra Pound, and calling notably often on Hugh MacDiarmid and Tom Scott as contributors, committed on sound Poundian principles to not seeing poetry in English in isolation from poetry in other tongues (hence, 'sipping Pernod' – though in fact *Agenda*'s foreign connections are more often Italian than French), remains to rival *The Review* long after it has been decisively outstripped in worldly terms. It remains the flea in Ian Hamilton's ear because William Cookson's historical perspective is longer than his – reaching back to the founding fathers of 'the modern movement', and loyal (now that Pound is dead) to such lonely survivors as MacDiarmid and David Jones. By contrast, Ian Hamilton's historical imagination reaches back no further than 1930; and his one attempt to account for an earlier monument, his essay on Eliot's 'Waste Land', has seemed – even to a sympathetic reader like his *Listener* reviewer, Alasdair Maclean – to be somehow missing the point.

In this foreshortening of the historical perspective Hamilton was following the precepts of one who for a long time seemed to be the mentor or avuncular presence behind *The Review*: A. Alvarez. The first issue of *The Review* featured (that seems to be the appropriate word) an unscripted dialogue between Alvarez and myself – an item which I am resigned to seeing described as 'famous' or 'sparkling' or 'memorable', though it was a notably unconsidered performance both on Alvarez's part and on mine. Like nearly everything else that ever appeared in *The Review*, it has been made to do double duty, and is readily available in a selection reprinted from the early issues of the magazine, entitled *The Modern Poet*. Accordingly, I am not going to give my impressions of it, beyond remarking that at one point I was trying to make us take our bearings from at least as far back as the generation of Pound and Eliot, and Alvarez was responding that that was all a long time ago and much water had flowed under the bridges since. Specifically, Alvarez tried (and failed) to get me to admit that Robert Lowell's translations were thoroughly in line with Pound's, and better; that, for practical purposes (so I interpret him), a study of Lowell would do as much for English poets of the 1960s as a study of Pound might have done. Ian Hamilton learned this lesson, and through most of the years of *The Review* Lowell was the standard by which other poets, British or American, were measured and found for the most part wanting. The first piece in *A Poetry Chronicle*, a review from 1965 of Lowell's *For the Union Dead*, puts the case as firmly as possible:

> There is no other poet writing at the moment who can match the dense visual accuracy of Lowell's best work; his concentration is insistently upon

'the stabbing detail', his intense demand is always for 'the universal that belonged to this detail and nowhere else' – nothing is inertly factual, nothing is neurotically corrupted; there is fever but no delirium. By an immensely subtle process of reverberation, his images seem to seek each other out, not to be wise so much as to be confirmed in tragedy, and they are interpenetrated in a structure tight enough to encompass their full range of connotation without any loss of urgency.

Hamilton has since condemned the Lowell who wrote *Notebook* – 'just rich enough to keep reminding us of what is being wasted'. He has not, so far as I know, committed himself to any opinion of the three interconnected Lowell collections published this year: *History, For Lizzie and Harriet, The Dolphin*.[1] Those who have read the devastatingly hostile review of these last in *The London Magazine*, a review by Geoffrey Grigson (whom *The Review* has in the past treated with great respect), will be agog to know Ian Hamilton's opinion of these volumes, particularly as they seem to represent no new development on Lowell's part but only a pushing further of the principles and practices that Hamilton found so admirable in *For the Union Dead*.

I return to 'the Varsity match', to Oxford's unbroken series of uncontested victories, to the match that will surely go down in history as 'Hamilton's', and so necessarily to the shorter historical perspective in which such parochial triumphs can figure large. Though plenty of people, especially self-congratulating Cambridge purists, envy Ian Hamilton his triumph, none of us has the right to do so: the rules and conditions of the game being as I have described

---

[1] I am told that Hamilton *has* committed himself on the latest Lowell collections, arguing that taken together they represent a recovery from *Notebook*.

them, he played the game more adroitly and patiently than his rivals, and so he has emerged as *victor ludorum*. Fair enough. One thing however we can ask of him: since his own career is best described (admittedly with some comic disproportion) in terms of *putsch* and brand-image and take-over bid, he ought not to use such terms with pejorative intent in describing the activities of others. Yet this is precisely what he does in a piece called 'The Making of the Movement' which, originally a brisk and accurate piece of journalism for a short-lived series of revaluations in the *New Statesman*, has already been reprinted once (in the Carcanet Press *British Poetry since 1960*) before re-appearing in *A Poetry Chronicle*, and may, for all I know, have enjoyed yet other leases of life in the U.S. or Australia or somewhere else in the English-speaking world.[1] Here, following a lead given by one of the Movementeers (as he acknowledges, though something less than handsomely), Hamilton decides, of the 1950s 'Movement': 'it was a take-over bid and it brilliantly succeeded'. So it was, and so it did. What else was *The Review*? And what else, what more, has it done?

After all one thing the Movement did was to hoist into prominence, and keep there, the poems of Philip Larkin. And Hamilton is content to be orthodox in admiring Larkin with very few reservations – in this, it is only fair to say, differing from Alvarez. It may be thought that in the 50s Larkin didn't need group-support; that he could have won his wide audience and his by now almost institutional status, unaided, on his own merits. One cannot prove this, nor disprove it. But the fact is that *The Less Deceived* was published not by Faber but by that institution of the Movement, George Hartley's Marvell Press. And it is

---

[1] It was, just to complicate matters, singled out in *Agenda* (by David Harsent) as having 'obvious (and immensely welcome) virtues'.

worth putting it on record that a version of that collection had earlier been rejected, by the Dolmen Press in Dublin. (The Irishmen who turned it down, Liam Miller, Sean White, Tom Kinsella, rejected Larkin for the same reason presumably as the Scotsman Tom Scott rejects him now – see Scott's letter in the *Listener*, 19th April 1973. Larkin's English admirers do not recognise how non-exportable he is, even within the British Isles.) In any case, whether or not Larkin *needed* support, he certainly got it – from Robert Conquest, George Hartley, John Wain. And what comparable collection has *The Review* group banded together to promote? The only possible candidate is Hamilton's own book of poems, *The Visit*, of which sure enough one of his *Review* team, Michael Fried, wrote that 'It is impossible to imagine a poetry more naked in its means or more lyrical in its essence. *The Visit* is a magnificent book, on a level with *Life Studies*, *Ariel* and *The Far Field*, and perhaps more exemplary than any of them.' And certainly *The Visit* was acclaimed not much less fervently than *A Poetry Chronicle* was to be. (The *T.L.S.* said that it 'marks an epoch'.) But there are no signs that it has found and held a following, as *The Less Deceived* did.

One of the most striking things about *The Review*, as a poetry magazine, is how little poetry it has printed. As I have suggested, its purpose was not to promote poets, but to promote critics, or rather, reviewers. Nevertheless in each issue the poems performed a crucial function; that they be few, and those few short, was very important. For this reinforced the harsh tone of the reviewing so as to create the illusion of critical rigour, of severe standards. The illusionism succeeded, and Ian Hamilton is now a by-word for severity. For 'grudging' read 'exacting', for 'narrow' read 'rigorous', for 'impatient' read 'fearless', and for 'hasty', 'urgent'. This too is a Varsity Match; Oxford's insouciance matched with Cambridge rancour, out of the defunct *Scrutiny*. The match was first made by Alvarez, when he reviewed poetry for the *Observer*; Hamilton learned it, and perfected it. In Alvarez and Hamilton alike, what emotional reality there is behind the effectively contrived posture is mostly *impatience*. 'One has to bear with . . .', 'one gets slightly weary of . . .' – these phrases (used of a poet whom in the end Hamilton grudgingly approves) are typical. *I WANT IT NOW*, a title from Kingsley Amis, is the motto that should stand at the head of Ian Hamilton's criticism, as of Alvarez's; they are the spokesmen for what, in Pound's words, 'The Age Demanded':

> *The 'age demanded' chiefly a mould in plaster,*
> *Made with no loss of time,*
> *A prose kinema, not, not assuredly, alabaster*
> *Or the 'sculpture' of rhyme.*

These are harsh words; to justify them, let readers compare, towards the end of *A Poetry Chronicle*, Hamilton's review of John Fuller's *The Tree that Walked* (old obligations have to be discharged!) with his review of MacDiarmid's *Collected Poems*. Or consider his irritated restiveness when confronted with Berryman's *77 Dream Songs*.

If literary London needs, for several years at a stretch, an arbiter of poetic taste (and apparently it does – once the arbiter was G. S. Fraser, then it was Alvarez, then it was Hamilton), could we have done worse, these last years, than have Ian Hamilton to put up with? Indeed we could; *much* worse. What is too seldom realised is that the prizes of this position are after all piffling – certainly in monetary terms, and even in terms of power. Who cares about poetry after all? Precious few. And this means that the people who scheme for this eminence, and in lucky cases get it, are after all men of principle; compromise as they must and do, still the motive behind their manoeuvres is a concern for poetry – that is to say, for what they understand as poetry, for that sort of poetry which they can respond to. To see the quagmire from which Fraser and Alvarez and Hamilton have lifted us, each in his turn, one need only look at the hapless young man in the *Sunday Times* who, entrusted with a poetry round-up every few weeks, finds each one of ten assorted poetry books a work of curious genius or great talent. There was a time (I can just remember it) when that sort of lax and beaming bonhomie was the order of the day; the hastiest and most wrongheaded discrimination is better than *that*, better than not discriminating at all.

But Hamilton in any case *has* talent, *has* courage, *has* integrity – though only Fuller perhaps would hail him as 'Most incorruptible of men'. He has other virtues. He is young enough to grow, and for good or ill to change his mind. He must have had an open or half-open mind about the Black Mountain poets when he got Charles Tomlinson to guest-edit a special issue on them; now he is implacable about them. Accordingly *The Review* is not monolithic first and last: *A Poetry Chronicle* includes a very hostile essay on Empson's poetry which is interestingly at variance with a special issue of *The Review* devoted to Empson, in which that least co-operative of interviewees hilariously frustrated the attempts of Christopher Ricks, his interviewer, to crown him with ceremonial laurel. And there are other instances of difference of opinion or change of opinion; differences and changes reflected sometimes in changes of personnel – Ricks and Gabriel Pearson and (most notably) Martin Dodsworth are ex-contributors whose possession of longer historical perspectives than Hamilton's seems to have made them quit his team. At any rate Hamilton is capable of learning from experience, and changing his mind.

He has another virtue which, though negative, is still welcome: he appears to have no political axe to grind. 'Do you . . . *sit?*' Thus I remember did A. Alvarez interrogate, with sudden access of gravity, Ian Hamilton and his companion when, in St. Pancras station, we all sat at lunch before proceeding to tape the far-famed dialogue between Alvarez and me. Already, I dare say, the question is indecipherable: it had to do with C.N.D., the Campaign for Nuclear Disarmament, and with its 'militant' wing, Bertrand Russell's Committee of 100, citizens who not only marched and shouted but defiantly sat down in the roadway at demonstrations, and gallantly forced the coppers to pull them out of the way. (I did not march, and wasn't even a member of C.N.D.; but, characteristically, no one asked.) As I recall, Hamilton and his friend replied with modest blushes that yes, *sit* was what they did. And that, I have always supposed, defined the political stance of *The Review*: left of centre, with a yawning opening towards the further Left; prepared to participate in the sub-politics of 'confrontation', but without much heart for it. If I am right, this interfered with Ian Hamilton's criticism hardly at all; an excessive indignation at Eliot's intellectual and social snobbery is the only sign of it that I can see in *A Poetry Chronicle*. Other contributors to *The Review* were not so circumspect: and in another place, for instance, I have remarked upon the alarming political guilelessness of Colin Falck.

Finally, Ian Hamilton *can* tell a hawk from a handsaw, when he allows himself time and space to do the job properly. Thus the best thing in *A Poetry Chronicle* is the longest item in it, a rambling essay, 'The Forties', in which he worries painstakingly about just what can be claimed for temporarily forgotten poets of the Second World War, like Alun Lewis, Julian Symons, Bernard Gutteridge.

When all is said and done, however, one is left wondering at the parochial self-regard which has somehow elevated *The Review*, a slim magazine at best, which seldom rewarded its subscribers with an issue according to the promised schedule, as a notable achievement of literary Britain in the 1960s. From any non-insular standpoint, *Agenda*, so much less vivacious and entertaining, has an infinitely better record. We really *are* a small nation, aren't we? And the Varsity Match won't soon be expunged from our social calendar.

Poetry Nation

'I shall try to get up to Orkney this summer if it can
be managed at all', Edwin Muir wrote to Kathleen
Raine from Cambridge, Massachusetts, on April 10,
1956. 'I suppose that what is wrong with me here is
that I am hungry. Horrible thought: I don't know
whether Eden was ever here.' Reading his letters, his
autobiography, *The Story and the Fable*, and almost
any of his poems, one realizes that, for him, the only
question about a place was whether Eden had been
there – and Eden meant his childhood in Orkney.
Although he makes much of this in his autobio-
graphy and his poetry, he scarcely mentions it in his
letters; and this only adds to the impression of his
exiled loneliness. He found an awareness of Eden in
Keats, Baudelaire, Goethe, Kafka, Rilke, Hofmanns-
thal, and in the music of Mozart, but in very little
contemporary writing in English. Inhabitants of
Eden were his friends John Holm and David Peat,
and, one supposes, his wife Willa Muir, though to
most visitors she appeared more like the angel with
the flaming sword guarding the gate. Apart from
Orkney, the places that qualified were Prague, Salz-
burg, Edinburgh: not Glasgow, nor London.

Muir was someone who had inhabited a green,
treeless, wonderfully light and shining island filled
with large solid objects, like sculpture, which were
people and animals, and – equally solid – myths and
moral qualities; and who had then moved into a
world outside that was, for the most part, foggy,
shadowy, threatening, evil, leaving him with nothing
of Eden but memories and vivid dreams. That other
world was – to use a word which he uttered quite
often and with intense literalness, as though seeing
the phenomenon it illustrated in front of him –
'dreadful'. In his scholarly biography of Muir, P. H.
Butter quotes a key passage:

When I was a child I must have felt that [my mother and father] had always been there, and I with them, since I could not account for myself; and now I can see them only as a stationary pattern, changing, yet always the same, not as a number of separate people all following the laws of their separate natures.

Muir adds that, until this impression was 'overlaid by later memories', his parents were 'fixed allegorical figures in a timeless landscape'.

His most basic belief was in immortality, though this belief was not attached to any religious dogma. He could sympathize with ratiocination that led to divine unreason, but it was, one feels, rather painful to him – embarrassing even. He was the opposite of someone who has to feel his way towards the supernatural. On the contrary, he felt himself departing from it; it was something he had relinquished. Moving from Orkney into a world which certainly unloaded on him plenty of its worries, he felt that there was some lack in him. In January 1940, when he was engaged on his autobiography, he wrote to Aleck Aiken, a mathematician who was also a lover of music and poetry:

Here am I, a middle-aged man and a professional writer and I have no philosophy. I had a philosophy when I was twenty-seven, but it was not my philosophy. I have no philosophy now – that is no rational scheme for accounting for all the time I have lived in the world, or comprehensively for life itself. And this lack – which I must share with several million people – really does dismay me, and gives me a troubling sense of insecurity. I believe that I am immortal, certainly, but that in a way makes it more difficult to interpret *this* life . . . I have no explanation, none whatever, of Time except as an unofficial part of Eternity – no historical explanation of human life, for the problem of evil seems insoluble to me: I can only accept it as a mystery, and what a mystery is I do not know.

Muir was consciously Keatsian in believing that there were mysteries bound up with human existence, and also in believing that one should remain in doubts and uncertainties about them. Like Keats, he lived in a world of what might be called pragmatic visions. He had strange dreams and waking visions, which he used to write down, and he looked to religion, not for dogmas, but to confirm in him the sense of the mysterious. Although he could see all the arguments for regarding mysteries as signs which led on towards a Church, a House of Sacred Rules, he couldn't pursue that path to its conclusion, any more than he could follow the signs of poverty and injustice of which he was so terribly aware (and which made him support socialism) up to the end which was the Church of Karl Marx. He writes to William Soutar:

> The theological dogmas do not help me; I can't digest them for my good; they're an obstacle to me (perhaps they shouldn't be but they are); and so I'm a sort of illicit Christian, a gate-crasher, hoping in my own way to slip in at David's hip yet. (February 3, 1940)

And he goes on in the same letter:

> The theory of the class struggle is based on a vision of history as wrath. Wrath may be the form of most history, but Marx makes wrath the very principle of good, or at least of advancement, and that is because his good and his advancement are purely historical.

It would be wrong to describe Muir as an out-

116

sider, or even as a loner. In a way he was part of the literary and intellectual establishment of his time – poet, novelist, translator, critic, British Council representative, frequenter of universities and PEN conferences. Nevertheless his letters read like the communications of someone who had left his own country and who is conscious, in nearly all his relationships, of frontiers which need to be crossed. He is constantly having to explain his origins, his current situation (he always gives the impression of being rather beleaguered), and his ideas, and continually trying to turn his life into a legend. He is happiest living in myth-enshrouded, almost heraldic, places where there are castles with impressive bastions and dark interiors (Salzburg, Prague, Edinburgh). Part of his legend (by which I mean, of course, his truth), as described in his autobiography, derives from the truly horrible experiences of his life after he had left the Orkney farm, and gone with his parents and two brothers to Glasgow. As he explained to H. L. Mencken (who had 'discovered' his book *We Moderns* in 1919):

I was born up [*sic*] in the Orkney islands in the north of Scotland, where my father was a small crofter. We all came to Glasgow when I was 14; my brothers, who were older than me, went into warehouses and I was sent into an office. Within four years, my father and mother and two brothers were dead, and I was left to fend for myself. Very bad health supervened for a while, and it was when I was emerging from it that Nietzsche came my way. (July 13, 1919)

Another terrible experience which Muir turned into legend was the appalling job that he took for two years in a bone-factory, 'a place where fresh and decaying bones, gathered from all over Scotland, were flung into furnaces and reduced to charcoal'.

Brought to London by his indomitable wife in 1919 at the age of thirty-two, Muir was in the position of having to press his credentials; he also closely examined the credentials of others. He acquired a considerable reputation as a critic, but, as these letters show, the standards by which he judged the work were very much those by which he judged the writer. He was true to his own instinctive good sense rather than to the intellectual values of critical detachment and objectivity. After his almost Wordsworthian education in the Orkney farm community, he had read widely, but he had no pretensions as an intellectual. He gives the impression in his letters of being a clear-minded, intelligent man who explores his own incorruptible taste.

The English writers of his time discussed in his early letters seem distinctly more foreign to him than Kafka or Thomas Mann. What really strikes him about England is that the conditions it imposes on the writer – even if better than those of a generation earlier – inevitably impoverished the literary result. In his early letters he discusses Lawrence, Joyce, Eliot, Wyndham Lewis, Lytton Strachey and Aldous Huxley, summing up his general attitude to them in a letter to Sydney Schiff:

> I would far rather live in this age which can show Joyce and *Ulysses*, than in the last one which could show nothing better than Shaw . . . I know the expense of spirit in this waste of shame which our generation is; the mysterious spiritual destruction of such really fine and gifted natures as Eliot, the spiritual twisting of Joyce, the distortion of everything, the chaos between the fall of one set of values and the discovery of another. (February 28, 1925)

He goes on to contrast 'the spiritual destruction' shown in writers of this generation with the poetic qualities discerned by Keats in his letters: 'As to the poetical character it lives in gusto, be it foul or fair, high or low, rich or poor, mean or elevated – it has as much delight in conceiving an Iago as Imogen'. Rather naively Muir complains of the lack of 'Sturm und Drang' in Lytton Strachey, adding: 'Because he disliked Sturm und Drang too much ever to over-come it, as the artist must, there is no joy.'

As a critic Muir was not what certain other critics are pleased to call 'dismissive'. He could admire the man of the gift and condemn the phenomenon. Thus, writing to Van Wyck Brooks about Aldous Huxley's *Antic Hay*, which he was evidently intending to re-view, he comments: 'It is fundamentally a very bad book very brilliantly done; no health from beginning to end: a very sad business; but I shall try to be fair' (January 28, 1924).

Thus, an emigrant from his Orkney Eden, Muir came to Hampstead in the early 1920s, and saw that the emperor had no clothes. With his conscious mind he could appreciate and admire the glitter and brilliance, while remaining aware of the nakedness underneath. He himself makes this distinction in his remarks on Wyndham Lewis: 'About Lewis, I have never come to satisfactory conclusions: except un-consciously, where I know I dislike him. . . .' The whole passage is as revealing of Muir as of Lewis:

I find him interesting – there are very few evil, positively evil, figures in our literature at present, and positive evil has an inspiring quality. But Lewis's evil strikes me as being the effect largely of a limitation: he does not seem to me to realise it: he strikes me in the very midst of it as being self-righteous, as imagining that he is right and all the world wrong. And on the other hand, there is no joy, no innocence, in his evil, as strangely enough, there seems to have been sometimes in literature. There is rather a sort of satisfaction at proving the whole world to be as unhappy as himself; the world is his enemy, and his satisfaction is to reduce it to humility. When is evil really great? When it is sublimely conscious of itself, as it was in Baudelaire and Dostoevsky; or when it is happily unconscious and innocent, as it was in Cellini and Stendhal. (May 8, 1925)

He criticizes London from a point of view which combines his own enisled provincialism (of another time as much as of another place), his travels to Salzburg and Prague, and his self-education in German and Central European, rather than Parisian, culture. The writers he was reading in 1924, when he was in Austria, were Thomas Mann, Schnitzler, Hofmannsthal and Georg Trakl.

Muir always had perceptions which cut through the work to what he sensed to be the moral condition of the author. As late as May 13, 1953, he writes to a student of Newbattle Abbey College (where he was teaching): 'The term is grinding on, and today I was talking about James Joyce. A writer to be admired (and sometimes enjoyed) but a sad chap altogether.' And he goes on: 'So much modern literature has come out of hatred, or disgruntlement, or what people call sophistication, which seems to me the most vulgar thing in the world. . . .'

To base criticism on values so personal is only significant if the writer retains throughout life what Herbert Read, whose Yorkshire farmhouse origins so remarkably parallel those of Muir, called 'the innocent eye'. Read himself, it might be said, though not losing his innocence, tended more and more to follow artistic fashion; Muir, on the other hand, was concerned not with the mysteriously changing values of art but with the solid, unchanging values of Orkney. He discovered traces of them in the castles of Salzburg and Prague, and in Kafka's *The Castle*, when he and his wife came to translate it. Muir responded to Kafka from the depths of his being. Nothing explains better what he expected from literature than his comments on *The Castle*:

> It is a purely metaphysical and mystical dramatic novel; the ordinary moral judgments do not come in at all; everything happens on a mysterious spiritual plane which was obviously the supreme reality to the author; and yet in a curious way everything is given solidly and concretely.

This combination of the metaphysical, mystical and spiritual with the solid and concrete was characteristic of Muir as well as Kafka; the comment reads like a summation of his own values. In a letter to me (May 4, 1935) he talks of writing poetry from the solidest basis within ourselves as the means of 'producing something that is new', and he states rather oddly, that he himself has to 'burst through to that solid foundation'. When he reaches it his poetry can surprise with his passion for authenticity, as when he exhorts himself, 'In a Time of Mortal Shocks',

> *Be closer*
> *Than the tongue-shaking lie is to the liar*
> *Lose to the loser.*
> *Be at the root*
> *No fear can find, the foot.*
> *There stay secure. . . .*
> *There is your house and keep your day.*

His letters are sensitive, intelligent, clear and completely truthful. At the same time they are less self-revealing than the passages of his autobiography about Orkney and the bone-factory.

One of the things which cannot be inferred even indirectly from Muir's letters is the effect his wife had on his relations with friends and employers. Willa Muir was warm, intelligent, entertaining, and

I have no doubt that she and Edwin loved one another deeply. However, she was one of those women who, on entering a room, seem to affect the scale of everything, and the relationships of everyone in it. Any difficulties, however slight, which her husband had in his job, were magnified into enormous grievances, and these made up a handsome quota of her vigorous, often witty conversation. With her Scottish accent, whose variations she played on freely to produce terrifying effects, she kept visitors to their Hampstead home in a state of nervous tension. She had something of the priestess about her, like the formidable Moneta in Keats's *The Fall of Hyperion*. But she was certainly a protective force as well as one who could hurl lightning. In their social duet, she was undoubtedly a dominant figure, and, with her in the room, little was heard from Edwin, unless through her, acting as a medium.

In contrast to his wife, Muir was like a very delicately balanced instrument of extreme sensitivity, uttering remarks of great intelligence in very pure tones. He describes in his letters a long poem called 'Chorus of the Newly Dead' which he began writing in 1924 and took up again in 1955. It seems to have been one of those efforts like Hoffmannsthal's *Das Kleine Weltheater*, which cover the whole of life in miniature. In his account of a draft of this poem he writes to Sydney Schiff:

I wish, accepting all these things, to affirm life, to use Nietzsche's expression. To do that it is necessary to realize the suffering first, to open my eyes to everything that seems hopeless, helpless, inexplicable. This, at least up to the figure of the harlot, is all that I have done thus far. The poet begins the new movement, away from suffering to its transmutation and the Hero emphasizes that movement; but I have another figure, I don't know what to call him, perhaps the Mystic, in which all life will be affirmed. Then there will be a grand final chorus. . . . (February 1, 1925)

Muir spent thirty years meditating on this theme. As a scenario, perhaps, it does not sound promising; but, with the concentration of every point of view within the vision of the mystic, it sounds remarkably like the story of his own inner life.

Times Literary Supplement

Poems from Magazines

Notice Prochorus Thompson. He has won
A competition with the smallest bones
In the whole churchyard. And the man-size grave
He shares with none tops all the tombstones.

Three months of life two hundred years ago.
From harvest time to ailing in November
He came to nothing much, even that Christmas
Not much for anybody to remember.

But little Prochorus Thompson bides his time.
He is the right length for sight-seers
Who pay no attention to the corpses
That lived for fifty, sixty speaking years.

Evergreen and rank are the paths between
The yew trees, and lichen creeps like evil
Over men who worked hard and dropped dead,
Women at menopause who saw the devil.

The balance of the churchyard must be righted.
May the full-grown dead seem interesting. May all
Children live longer than Prochorus Thompson.
Strangle the church tower and the passing bell.

Poetry Book Society Supplement

After so many sessions of ice and fire
To regain at the end of them some peace of mind,
I had hoped to meet you my only daughter
With a sense of the nakedness of an open hand.
And of finding in talk, as I do, the familiar
References, not to what has been, but to what is,
As if we shared at least some colour
Of saying, quietly now, without intensities,
Words that were both strange and strangely
    familiar.

But, as usual, it is not the expected that happens;
You go round with a crowd you met in Majorca,
And the gulf, by meeting, is not bridged but deepens
And I do not know who you were or who you are.
But listen as strangeness its knife sharpens
On all the varieties of impotent chatter,
Feeling the gulf between us, as it widens,
And how far you are from the heart of the matter,
Which I do hear beating though no one else listens,
And it is trouble, indeed, of an extreme fervour,
As you skate on thin ice which, though it glistens,
Is the thinnest possible skin above danger.

But I know that the way is in the waiting
In silence, though even that is a threat to her,
Whose heart I catch erratically beating
Under the tricks designed for a crowded parlour.
But it is all I understand of a possible meeting,
Though your grief I sense like a diviner,
And the sound of a lost child somewhere crying
Under the songs you sing and the ersatz laughter.

Meridian

And it will happen one day,
Or you, or I will not be travelling our mutual way,
But one, so it seems, distant and far
From this abiding place that we now share.
I wonder, though, perhaps some trick of the mind
But makes us seem deaf, dumb, senseless and blind,
Intangible, for we, without such senses
Already have proved here our substances
Are not the only way of being together,
Though far apart, still been with one another.
So, all is well, and all will still be well;
The burning, a trick of the mind, the tolling bell;
A pause, till one 'There was no need to bother,
We were not ever absent from each other.'

Aquarius

My dancing is, in my opinion, good,
In the right, cramped circumstances, and provided
Other people are too preoccupied with
Their own to notice mine. I am happy
To have lived into an informal age when
Standing and shaking in approximate rhythm, not
Bowing and guiding, is the idea. Because to
Have to know regulated steps and be skilful was
        what
I could never manage at all when it was the thing.

So I do dance. But I'm never entirely sure.
It's a kind of movement you would never make
In the normal course, and how much it always
        seems
To obtrude on the natural in an embarrassing
Way wherever people get it started!
Set it apart, on a stage, with a large
Orchestra, it's all right, it's undoubtedly clever,
And the costumes are glorious to gawp at, but
It still looks a little bit foolish, moving like *that*?

To speak of how all its origins are so
Utterly primal – the planets, the seasons,
The rhythms of mating, and so on, and so on,
Is to list a lot of fundamental things,
Explain them, and exorcise dancing:
Because simply why dance if you've come to
        understand
What dancing mimes so roughly, or makes such
A repetitive pantomime of? Sleights of courtship,
Postures of delight, grief, vanity, idolatry I see

All around me more sharp and subtle for not being
Done in a style. Dancing has social uses,
I know, but so did elemental spears and punches
        before

They invented tables for eating and conducting
Verbal negotiation (and does hands
Gripping slyly under a table ever happen
In the middle of a fandango?)
Moreover, if the elemental stuff
Of dancing is banal, the ancient, ritual and
customary

Panoply of 'the dance' is incredibly peculiar:
Fellows in feathers, or kilts, or puma-skins,
Guys trinkling little bells down there in
Hampshire,
Or folding arms over black boots flicking in the
Urals . . . one surely turns away to find somewhere
quieter,
Where one needn't be part of a silly circle
Of grips, clapping hands in moronic unison (I once
Took a pocket torch in, to go on reading – the
Listener,
I believe – all the way through a Gene Kelly musical.)

For ostensible moralist reasons, the
Puritans disliked dancing; but they also
Opposed all giving and wearing of jewellery,
In which they may well have been right; so, with
dancing,
They may also have come at the truth
From a wrong, religious direction. But, down
Oxford Street
These days, whatever the mortgage rate, there
jogs
In shine or rain an irrelevant group of chanters
Shuffling to the rhythm of tiny cymbals, opposing

Shaven sublimity to the big, crude, selling
Metropolis around; and *dancing*, in sandals, for
converts.
They'd like to see everyone join them . . . how
unlikely,

I think; and how such unlikelihood shows
That most of us only don or discard our
Finery, to dance, in a fit of social desperation.
I recall that outside the Hammersmith Palais,
There was once an illuminated sign announcing
A group of performers known as THE SANDS OF
TIME.

For months, the words, I surmised, were a motto
Of that establishment: a thousand grains shaken
Nightly in that vast box, a thousand softies
Sifting for life-partners as the hours and days
Ticked on in tawdry, implacable rhythms. Yet the
Dancing prospers – telling how many the world
     leaves
Despoiled of words, of gestures diverse and
     specific,
Of shades of forehead, or hintings of finger-tips,
Or any more delicate tremor that speaks the whole
     thing;

And this is the crux. Tides vary, exact shelvings
Of pebbles on shores don't repeat, while patterns
     of clouds
Are never the same, are never *patterns*. Raindrops,
At unforeseen moments run, and weigh, down,
     minutely,
A million particular grass-blades: movement,
     movement,
Everlastingly novel shifts of a universe not
Gracelessly ordered, not presided by a setter of
Regulations. Vanity is so sad pretending to
     represent
Nature with humans dancing. Those who can move
     need not dance.

Critical Quarterly

Overtaking a mustard van belonging to the
    gasboard,
overtaking a lorry with asbestos roofing,
some sharp peaked, some curved, leaping on a plank
    back,
stuck behind a tarmac lorry, T patterning olive paint
    like a chinese jug.

Overtaking a black lorry, nameplate obliterated with
    mud
tail lights purpled, differential dangling like a dirty
    udder,
tiny chain chinking from the strip of metal slotted
    to keep the let down back up.

Overtaking a volvo, smooth creamy paint
reflecting the nodding dog in the back,
soft rubber flaps with 'volvo' on them guarding the
    back tyres,
driver's spectacles in the driving mirror,

Overtaking an empty cattle truck smelling of
    farmyard,
stuck behind a swaying tree trunk with a white rag
    flickering warning over the annual rings,
overtaken by a ford with a draught of radio music
    and a smiling executive face,
overtaken by an austinful of children who toss
    papers into butterflies,
overtaken by a zephyr with a blonde in the passenger
    seat who turns into a long eared dog in passing,

stuck behind a caravan jerking on its tow,
red and white check curtains flapping through open
    windows,

stuck behind a bus, behind a truck, behind a petrol
tanker, behind a
milkfloat, behind a tractor, behind a lorry, loaded
with a mysterious parcel
roped under green canvas, and no chance of turning
off or overtaking for ten miles.

Omens

When I got there cattle were standing around.
Their colour drained as light slipped over the hills
And they showed as white patches, mainly. The pond
Was edged with the deep pits of their walking
But now they were still as trees, just ears and tails
Spasmodically flicking.

The water was polished like a sheet of zinc
And stiff hair reeds pierced it in bunches.
I tackled up, knotting by torchlight; my feet sank
In the cattle treads as I threw the spoon
And reeled it back, controlling its flutters and lunges
Over hidden weed and stone.

I was almost surprised by the splash and scatter
Of ripples as the spoon went in, by the reminder of
      wet.
The surface had been so flat that a clatter,
An uncompromising meeting of metals, a test
Of temper, would not have seemed inappropriate
At that first cast.

The water yielded, though, as water will.
There was the soft reassurance of bubbles; the line
      dripped.
The spoon travelled easily to the hiss of my reel
With only the friction of silk, less noise than a
      breath.
My foothold locked in the ruts and I stopped
Sinking, held in the earth.

Darkness came and sat on the whole scene.
Without my noticing, the cattle wandered away.
The water went black and was without reflection.
Had I let the surface settle, possibly a star
Would have swum there, but I was too busy
For that manoeuvre.

Nothing was any good. The pond grew strange
Again. After an hour's empty work
I could feel its deliberate change
From a cell of sleek and self-renewing life
To a black volcanic sterile hole in the rock.
Its deadness stilled belief.

The lights of a slow plane came moaning
A couple of miles above me. You always find
People with somewhere to get to. Leaning
Into the bend of the rod I cast again,
Taking a purposeful stance, but the pond
Could have stood on stone.

I made no contact with anything in the dark.
No muscular shape came twisting out of the pond.
Not even a scrap of weed stuck to the hook.
And I knew that every cast would be in vain
And that I should go on casting till the wind
At dawn brought up the rain.

Workshop New Poetry

John Cassidy   **Hill Mist**

The sheep cries were echoless,
unclear. That was the first thing.
Peaks stark a minute before
were gone now, and the colour
in the grass had been switched off,
half-noticed; but the sudden
dead sound of the bleating spelt
open threat. The rest followed.

Hardly had I resented
the clasp of cold on my neck
than the mist stood solidly
everywhere, almost nudging
my shoulder to stagger me
into peat pools, feet baffled,
unsure of anything, the
very ground untrustworthy.

Getting down out of it was
not the easiest of skills.
There was a full beck running
loud enough to be found if
I wanted to try. Never
follow a river, follow
a wall. Rivers can become
cataracts and rope down cliffs.

You see them streaking the sides
of hills, often the only
glitter in a grey day, loud,
silver and suicidal.
They have a logic that I
hesitate at, a straight-down
get-there determination.
It is the way of water.

But men build walls; they lumber
boulders in incredibly
precarious places, they
manage a balance you can
only gasp at, but where men
have lodged and perched stones there is
a sureness, a sense of place,
and other men find foothold.

Dare as they did and you can
trust them, moving with caution,
palms running over rough grain,
lichen, tufts of wool where sheep
have jumped, reassuring loaf-
shapes settled with so precise
an art, such knowledgeable
hands, that they live as comrades.

Grope for a wall then, wander
stride after slow stride towards
a loom of stone, past sheep skeined
in condensed mist, still, stopping
their chewing to watch you pass.
They turn their horned, alien
heads and stare. This is their world.
Bracken tangles your ankles.

It was as it always is.
The wall was there, in the end,
pushing itself in my path.
I caught hold of it, followed
its side as it led downward,
and came to the valley like
an awakening. Bright fields
were thick with hay being worked.

In the warm smells I walked through
there was friendliness; farmers
asked how it had been on top.
Damp, I said, looking back up
where the slope edged into cloud
and the walls vanished. It was
a word for the difference,
a word. I shook myself dry.

Not far away the rattle
of water flourished again
the river's dash from the crag
and its jovial bounce through
the valley's acres. That free
drop sparkled and surged in my
head all day. The wall's art, too,
was something I was glad of.

Stand

John Cassidy   **An Attitude of Mind**

Heat bounced off the cobbled yard
And hit us in the eyes, already bleared
By the sun to a constant blink.
Starlings showered down onto the barn,
Dipped through the door, paused, and sprayed up
    again,
Ceaselessly. Dust twirled slowly; a tractor stank.

Tod took a tennis racket, and flicked
It from hand to hand. You've picked
A good time, he said. I'll demonstrate.
The barn was heavy with hay smell
And all in it invisible
When Tod swung the doors together, tight.

139

In the dimness hovered small echoings,
The whirring motors of starlings' wings,
Soft and confusing, and right up,
Where the nests were, raucous twitters.
We stood till things assembled round us,
Colouring themselves and taking shape:

A spiked machine, blue plastic sacks
Of nitro-chalk, a couple of hayforks,
A three-wheeled pram. Heavy beams
Hung over us, streaked white like the walls
Up at the top amid squalls
Of bird noise. Tod flung wide his arms

And shook his muscles loose, and took
A good grip on his racket. With a kick
He broke some pebbles free, and flung one
Up at the roof, then another, then more,
And they clunked about on the wood up there
Before the sharp drop back onto stone.

And down came the starlings, beating about
In a bewildered way, at head height and waist
    height,
Dozens of them, whizzing so close they missed
Us by the width of their wind. Tod was using
The racket, swinging from the shoulder, not pausing
At all, grunting and moving very fast.

Blow after blow vibrated those strings.
Bodies rocketed to stillness, and there were
    shufflings
And dragging movements everywhere,
As birds, beaks broken, necks half-unscrewed,
Flapped untidily and slowly clawed
A small circular progress on the floor.

Tod stamped on these but others escaped to the roof
In the end and sat safe. Tod gave a laugh
At his last few futile swipes and looked
Round at the litter of feathers, at the wrecks
Of birds and bits of birds, at the marks
On the walls where birds had split and cracked.

The nearest bodies he nudged with the toe of his
      boot
To a neat heap, and he scooped with his racket
Several more to throw in; he was deft, accurate.
Hungry nests wheezed still. They'll soon starve,
That lot, Tod said, stroking his ear with the curve
Of his racket. Tomorrow in here will be dead quiet.

He opened the doors and the daylight fell
In, hot and dazzling. A good haul,
He said, licking sweat, wiping an eye, puzzled
At my silence. Pests they are from the minute they
      hatch.
It's all an attitude of mind. He raised an arm to
      scratch.
Down the words Dunlop Junior dark blood drizzled.

B.B.C. Radio 3

John Cotton   **Kilroy was Here**

'English had as his second-in-command of artillery another American, a man named Bradish, whose name can be seen now cut into the altar in the inner sanctuary at Abu Simbel. Little else is known of him.' *The Blue Nile*: Alan Moorehead.

Remember me:
the burden of Dido's lament;
and of those names we see
written or carved
in sometimes improbable places?
Well, the names are there
if not the faces.
Certainly it would seem true
of Bradish's self-cut memorial.
Against the fear
of nothingness
I was here
plead all the Kilroys of this world:
Alexander's soldier
who left his Greek in Northern India,
and Desaix's men
who inscribed Dendera.
Then those suitably ephemeral
declarations of affection,
hearts and names
scratched on cactus leaves
on a cliff path in Spain:
Hans unt Beyb;
Teresa y Fernando;
and, touching in its mild chauvinism,
May and Bert, England.

Outposts

Ian Crockatt **Roundabout**

1. *Bravado*

All brats are bog-full of filth – it's a state
of mind, or a lack of mind more likely.
But no cauldron of toads beats a baby
for sheer Ugh! they make a fetish of it.
To hear them bawling their nappies off at
bag-eyed parents in cafes, shops, or see
them bald as plums in swampy prams, clearly
good for nothing except noise and shit –
and God, they screech and ooze like that all night –
is to confirm that no monstrosity,
no embryonic bag of din and pee,
will ever warp the womb of my bed-mate!
Give me the cauldron, the toady brews
and smells anyday, but birth – that's Bad News!

2. *New Moon*

The moon starts up. She's taut with our miracle,
I'm silent – there's little to shout about,
we're old hands, we've read all the articles,
it's our second time round this roundabout.
We lie like this, wide-eyed, most nights, feeling
beneath us the same sheets and the same bed,
the same house, garden, the same earth spinning
that last year mocked us with a son born dead.

Hope and fear prostrate our structured pride.
We're on our knees begging you Mother Earth
for this life – bury the hatchet that buried
us then, make this an ordinary birth!
Night digests our prayer. She breaks, I lie
too close to doubt to speak. The moon creaks by.

3. *Like a father*

Your lungs lie wrinkled, unswollen by air,
but already I listen for crying.

Like a father I dream, imagining
my dreams will crowd your mind, all realised there,
Wanting to warn you, I plot each mistake
of my own half-life, plan great lives for you;
already you and I have laughed lives through
together, have spun worlds in our wake . . .
I'd laugh at myself if I wasn't so scared.
O my half-child, I want so much for you,
from you, that you might never give or take!
Be born! Let your lungs swell and your cry declare
that sure, emphatic life inhabits you,
and live, in spite of me, for your own sake!

4. Stone-talk

It's dead, forget it. Stripped down, shoved back in
the brain and lost, it can't hurt, forget it.
What's to remember? The wife sick and swollen
with fear, half-hopes, a cracked dream – forget it.
So a world's collapsed – who cares? I'm hard, flint
on a dead world's crust, and anything goes –
and if some soft jerk mourns me, or blinks a hint
of shock, so what? it's no skin off my nose.
Mother earth! What a crude, cockteasing bitch
of a world it is, what a ragbag of taunts
and callousness, what a whore – God it haunts
itself with failure and blood this whore . . . Bitch,
bitch of the pimping moon, curse, writhe about
and I won't crawl, I'm stone – you've ground me out.

5. Ways, Words

Buried in bed, in sheets buried, in bed –
O bed of loss, of lust, of love, unloose
sheets of love, burier of lust, of loss,
let love's way, love's word, crowd this spinning head.

Till then blood, no crying, no crying. World
of cauldron's toad, of whore and fleet spawning,
let seed find ways, find words of forgetting,

seed's way, seed's word, crowd where death has
   curled.

Eyewhite moon coldly circles our each night
and O the lilywhite worlds we create.
Let time teach ways, teach words of forgetting.

Blackeyed earth spins indifferent as night
O the life and the love, the crying, the hate.
Let grief learn ways, learn words of forgetting.

6. *Bravado*

Workshop New Poetry

You've got it made:
they hang to your pauses,
the questions your host feeds to you.
Because you're

THE MAN

A few easy openers about the early days,
how you began;
the vaudeville act with your sister
— you supporting her.
                              Then
the move to broadway, the shows, films.

Feint surprise as he asks you to sing;
'Cheek to Cheek'
'Putting on the Ritz'
                              — applause each time.
But
    when, larger than life, your image
fills the screen behind you,
top hat, tails and cane weave a memory.
                                          That
is the real thing:
                    the breathless grin,
hands waving-like a magician's:
                                      feet
machine-gunning the beat
as if the hands held strings.
You vault chairs and tables;
piano and bar are props around which
you spin the number.

Finally, as all had anticipated,
he coyly challenges you to dance.

seventy, wrinkled neck like bark,
you take the cue.
                              The band's plushness
now serves to cover the dulled edge of your tapping.
Satisfied, the audience applauds
the length of the credits:
was worth the price to say:

          'I saw Astaire dance.'

                              They
carry the movie image home in their minds,
nostalgic tunes all the way,
blind to the varicose veins, ignoring the toupé.

                                        Poetry Wales

> *— And Paradiso? Is there a*
> *paradise?*
> *— I think so, madam,*
> *but nobody wants sweet wines*
> *any more.*
> Eugenio Montale, translated
> by G. Singh

Not so fast, waiter.
If there are those who like sweet wine
And have earned the price of it,
Then they should have it.

Plonk will do for me.
If there's cork in it
Or lipstick on the rim,
I shan't make a fuss.
Some of us will be lucky to get vinegar
Pushed at us.

But for others
You had better be ready to serve sweet wine
In clean glasses, unchipped,
And without a speech.
Some customers are by definition
Right,
As it happens,
And do not require to be told
About a fine dry wine
Deriving from individually crushed grapes
Grown on a certain slope on a small hill
Overlooking a distinguished river.

Some of your customers
Have already been individually crushed.
They know dryness in the mouth,
A harsh taste at the back of the throat.
If sweet wine is what they fancy
You will give them sweet wine.

And there should be room on your tray
For ginger-beer, orangeade, cocoa, tea
And even the vulgar vintage of colas.

London Magazine

Gavin Ewart   **Sonnet: Mother Love**

Women are always fond of growing things.
They like gardening; snipping, watering, pruning,
bringing on the backward, aware of the forward;
planting – not for nothing do they talk of 'nurseries'.
Roses are like children, a source of pride,
tulips are cosseted, primulas are pets.
These are almost as loved as the usual surrogates –
the dogs and cats that stand for families.

Conservation, preservation; it's a lovable aspect
of maternalism (one reason why we're here).
Better than that, this severe matriarchy
is established over *plants*; the bossiness, thank God,
that puts you there (delphiniums), you there
     (wallflowers),
is harmlessly deflected well away from us.

London Magazine

Fourth of October 1973:
I pick the date to form a line of these
Iambics that keep falling in in threes.

Future historians, and epistolists
On cyclic weather patterns to *The Times*,
May note that I still wore a summer suit.

The bloody oblong that the creeper seems
Beyond the lavatory's striated pane
Astonishes the calls of nature still.

Its life, however, must be told in days.
And even Auden, unforgettable
Because of his creativeness, begins

To fade as what he was: the body – loved,
Or awesome but indifferent natural object –
Breaks up beneath the top-soil of Kirschstetten.

The tractor crawls along – is making! – that
Curved difference between the green and brown
Upon the tilted upland. Here is what

Essential memory depends upon.
For if the plough should fail, the superstructure
Collapses. Howard Newby tells me that

The night of Auden's death he was himself
In Vienna, near that fatal-roomed hotel,
Not knowing Auden there, still less his end.

As what he was. In spite of Howard's health,
Comparative youth, quite soon none will recall
What Auden's 'world' was like when first created.

Autumn: the leaf more insecurely hangs
Than hung the fruit. Nights longer. Weather worse.
Noise of the rain brings other noises near.

Can we love retrospectively the dead
We never really knew? I start to think so;
Especially since there is no question of

Unwished for or unrequited love. And now
The blood's all trickled to the ground; the voice
Only on tape; speculatively warm the clasp.

The Listener

1.

The sheep has stopped crying.
All morning in her wire-mesh compound
On the lawn, she has been crying
For her vanished lamb. Yesterday they came.
Then her lamb could stand, in a fashion,
And make some tiptoe cringing steps.
Now he has disappeared.
He was only half the proper size,
And his cry was wrong. It was not
A dry little hard bleat, a baby-cry
Over a flat tongue, it was human,
It was a despairing human smooth Oh!
Like no lamb I ever heard. Its hindlegs
Cowered in under its lumped spine,
Its feeble hips leaned towards
Its shoulders for support. Its stubby
White wool pyramid head, on a tottery neck,
Had sad and defeated eyes, pinched, pathetic,
Too small, and it cried all the time
Oh! Oh! staggering towards
Its alert, baffled, stamping, storming mother
Who feared our intentions. He was too weak
To find her teats, or to nuzzle up in under,
He hadn't the gumption. He was fully
Occupied just standing, then shuffling
Towards where she'd removed to. She knew
He wasn't right, she couldn't
Make him out. Then his rough-curl legs,
So stoutly built, and hooved
With real quality tips,
Just got in the way, like a loose bundle
Of firewood he was cursed to manage,
Too heavy for him, lending sometimes
Some support, but no strength, no real help.

153

When we sat his mother on her tail, he mouthed her
    teat,
Slobbered a little, but after a minute
Lost aim and interest, his muzzle wandered,
He was managing a difficulty
Much more important and urgent. By evening
He could not stand. It was not
That he could not thrive, he was born
With everything but the will –
That can be deformed, just like a limb.
Death was more interesting to him.
Life could not get his attention.
So he died, with the yellow birth-mucus
Still in his cardigan.
He did not survive a warm summer night.
Now his mother has started crying again.
The wind is oceanic in the elms
And the blossom is all set.

2.

The mothers have come back
From the shearing, and behind the hedge
The woe of sheep is like a battlefield
In the evening, when the fighting is over,
And the cold begins, and the dew falls,
And bowed women move with water.
Mother mother mother the lambs
Are crying, and the mothers are crying.
Nothing can resist that probe, that cry
Of a lamb for its mother, or an ewe's crying
For its lamb. The lambs cannot find
Their mothers among those shorn strangers.
A half-hour they have lamented.
Shaking their voices in desperation.
Bald brutal-voiced mothers braying out,
Flat-tongued lambs chopping off hopelessness.
Their hearts are in panic, their bodies
Are a mess of woe, woe they cry,
They mingle their trouble, a music

Of worse and worse distress, a worse entangling
They hurry out little notes
With all their strength, cries searching this way and
    that.
The mothers force out sudden despair, blaaa!
On restless feet, with wild heads.
Their anguish goes on and on, in the June heat.
Only slowly their hurt dies, cry by cry,
As they fit themselves to what has happened.

The Listener

Ted Hughes   **Swifts**

Fifteenth of May. Cherry blossom. The swifts
Materialise at the tip of a long scream
Of needle – 'Look! They're back! Look!' And they're
        gone
On a steep

Controlled scream of skid
Round the house-end and away under the cherries.
        Gone.
Suddenly flickering in sky summit, three or four
        together,
Gnat-wisp frail, and hover-searching, and listening

For air-chills – are they too early? With a bowing
Power-thrust to left, then to right, then a flicker they
Tilt into a slide, a tremble for balance,
Then a lashing down disappearance

Behind elms.
                    They've made it again,
Which means the globe's still working, the
        Creation's
Still waking refreshed, our summer's
Still all to come –
                            And here they are, here they are
                            again
Erupting across yard-stones
Shrapnel-scatter terror. Frog-gapers,
Speedway goggles, international mobsters –

A bolas of three or four wire screams
Jockeying across each other
On their switchback wheel of death.
They swat past, hard-fletched,

Veer on the hard air, toss up over the roof
And are gone again. Their mole-dark labouring,
Their lunatic limber scramming frenzy
And their whirling blades

Sparkle out into blue –
                              Not ours any more.
Rats ransacked their nests, so now they shun us.
Round luckier houses now
They crowd their evening dirt-track meetings

Racing their discords, screaming as if speed-burned,
Head-height, clipping the doorway
With their leaden velocity and their butterfly
    lightness,
Their too-much power, their arrow-thwack into the
    eaves.

Every year a first-fling nearly-flying
Misfit flopped in our yard,
Groggily somersaulting to get airborne.
He bat-crawled on his tiny useless feet, tangling his
    flails,

Like a broken toy, and shrieking thinly
Till I tossed him up – then suddenly he flowed away
    under
His bowed shoulders of enormous swimming power,
Slid away along levels wobbling

On the fine wire they have reduced life to,
And crashed among the raspberries.
Then followed fiery hospital hours
In a kitchen. The moustached goblin savage

Nested in a scarf. The bright blank
Blind, like an angel, to my meat-crumbs and flies.
Eyelids resting. Wasted clingers curled.
The inevitable balsa death.

                    Finally burial
              For the husk
              Of my little Apollo —

              The charred scream
              Folded in its huge power.

                                                The Listener

Once, as a child, I ate raspberries. And forgot.
And then, years later,
A raspberry flowered on my palate, and the past
Burst in unfolding layers within me.
It tasted of grass and honey.
You were there, watching and smiling.
Our love unfolded in the taste of raspberries.

More years have passed; and you are far, and ill;
And I, unable to reach you, eating raspberries.
Their dark damp red, their cool and fragile fur
On the always edge of decay, on the edge of bitter,
Bring a hush of taste to the mouth

Tasting of earth and of crushed leaves,
Tasting of summer's insecurity,
Tasting of crimson, dark with the smell of honey,

Tasting of childhood and of remembered childhood,
And now, now first, the darker taste of dread.

Sap and imprisoned sunlight and crushed grass
Lie on my tongue like a shadow,
Burst like impending news on my aching palate

Tasting not only of death (I could bear that)
But of death and of you together,
The folded layers of love and the sudden future,
Tasting of earth and the thought of you as earth

As I go on eating, waiting for the news.

New Statesman

Alasdair Maclean   **In Time of 'The Breaking of Nations'**

It's in the corners of the galleries one finds them,
where it's dark,
those old Dutch genre paintings,
hung there in Victorian days
after so many vapourings and faintings,
after such loosening of stays.
For in them nearly always,
as one's guarantee,
some peasant has held up his game of bowls
and quite without remark
walked off to pee.

Not far, of course.
It isn't delicacy he has in view.
The nearest bit of shady wall will do
where he may lean and cool his forehead
while he waits for confirmation to come through.
Indeed, for the better savouring of this hour
he has topped up his bladder well beyond its
    measure.
His muscles seal the opening an exquisite moment
    more
then 'Ah!' he goes 'Ah!' in sheer pleasure.

Good luck to him!
I think that in a world
where bigger heads come daily in on platters
he is his own continuation
for he has grasped what matters.
It pleases me to see him there
while in the same painting
but under a different sky
Napoleon or whatever his name was then
thunders helplessly by.

London Magazine

Derek Mahon   **A Refusal to Mourn**
               (*for Maurice Leitch*)

He lived in a small farmhouse
At the edge of a new estate.
The trim gardens crept
To his door, and car engines
Woke him before dawn
On dark winter mornings.

All day there was silence
In the bright house. The clock
Ticked on the kitchen shelf,
Cinders moved in the grate,
And a warm briar gurgled
When the old man talked to himself;

But the doorbell seldom rang
After the milkman went,
And if a coat-hanger
Knocked in an open wardrobe
That was a great event
To be pondered on for hours

While the wind thrashed about
In the back garden, raking
The roof of the hen-house,
And swept clouds and gulls
Eastwards over the lough
With its flap of tiny sails.

Once a week he would visit
An old shipyard crony,
Inching down to the road
And the blue country bus
To sit and watch sun-dappled
Branches whacking the windows

While the long evening shed
Weak light in his empty house,
On the photographs of his dead
Wife and their six children
And the Missions to Seamen angel
In flight above the bed.

'I'm not long for this world'
Said he on our last evening,
'I'll not last the winter',
And grinned, straining to hear
Whatever reply I made;
And died the following year.

In time the astringent rain
Of those parts will clean
The words from his gravestone
In the crowded cemetery
That overlooks the sea
And his name be mud once again

And his boilers lie like tombs
In the mud of the sea bed
Till the next ice age comes
And the earth he inherited
Is gone like Neanderthal Man
And no records remain.

But the secret bred in the bone
On the dawn strand survives
In other times and lives,
Persisting for the unborn
Like a claw-print in concrete
After the bird has flown.

New Statesman

I try to tune in, but Europe's blurred voice
Becomes stranger with the movement of the dial.

All stations seem to give a fragment of
Performance – Mozart disarmed by a fizzled
Prodigy; innumerable cliques of wordsmiths.

As the electric crackles I make believe
I am composing an avant-garde symphony,
A sound poem for a hall of idiot speech.

But behind the static are moments of sanity:
A string quartet and interesting chanteuse;
Then histrionics at a play's climax.

For some reason, a hubub of languages
And dim music becomes more important
Than any scheduled programme. It suits

My mood perhaps, this indecipherable mayhem
Of newscasters and sopranos, and the long
Returns to electronic gibbering.

Somewhere, behind a rockband's sudden squall,
A morse message is tapped out. For a few seconds
It is clear, articulate, before melting

Into Europe's verbiage. It was not mayday.
And I twist the dial a hairsbreadth into jazz.

Poetry Wales

We have been pacing the precincts.
We are worried in unison.
We wonder what the hero is doing.
We never understood heroes.
We do not entirely believe the messenger.
The hero's mother seems perturbed.
On the other hand, the king is silent.
What is obscure is seldom clear.
We were not born in this country.
Who is that coming towards us?
Is it a man? Is it a woman?
It is the oracle. Once the oracle
has spoken, we shall be more doubtful.
In our country there are no oracles.
We are sorry today for ourselves.
But it is not for us to complain.
The king, we may say, is irascible.
Already perhaps we have said too much.
To say too much is always too often.
Here we are at the foot of the steps.
Let us all be silent in unison
and hear what the oracle has to tell us.

The oracle says, 'When winter comes
the autumn is over.' Are we comforted?
We do not know if we like winter.
We wonder what the gods are doing.
We never understood gods.

Akros

John Ormond **Boundaries**
            (*for Peter Tinniswood*)

A black flag giving assent to spring's
Illumination of the book of hours,
The whiteness of my almond tree; in anthracite
Of feathers, this blackbird singing.

Each evening just before dusk, in festival,
His pertinent cadenza to the day
Defines his territory, marks his boundary
Under my work-room window. The pane,

A yard or two of air, that's all there is
Between us. All? Yellow flute, black performer,
He flaunts his beginner's luck, chiding, gliding
Through variations upon unfound themes;

His musical unconcern crucial
To the seeming accident of song,
His obbligato signature deriving
From ancestries of whistling, unanimous

With the blossom. He, hero of branches,
(Trick of his head) perpetually surprised
To be trapped inside what he whistles,
Inventing nothing, being invention,

Flawless as makes no matter, taunting me
To delight. He essays yes out of his history
Against all configurations of silence
Through the one throat he happens to have.

Evening adjusts the trance of sky. His spate
Of acrobatics on a three-line stave,
Sardonic, repetitious, can never be whole
Except as part of what I wish to be whole.

Music to him is custom. His easy tricks
Are my despair. I turn back to the page
Where my chantepleure is born already broken.
What can I bid against him but misère?

And yet the future is still to be done.
He stabs me broad awake with notes
Not of his whistling. Thus runs spring's rigmarole
With no song substitute for any other.

Poetry Wales

It was for this they were made,
The great present of their childhood
Kept unopened, the hard rules obeyed
And the grudged honey of being good:
A pure reward,
Better for being stored,
And, reached at last, seeming like the sea
Stretching after a dream of ice toward
The edge of reluctance turbulently.

So that the stunned moment now
When talk falls in the bright marquee
Is an elevation of hope, the drinks a vow
Naming everything which is to be;
And after this
The subtly twinned kiss
To start a carnal journey, and the night
Offering shining emphasis
Like crystal gifts emboldening the light.

To which the cynical, caught up
In the flurry of guy ropes let down
And crushed flowers in delicate cups,
Pay tribute as sexual clowns:
After this huge
Joke, a terrible deluge
The speeding innocents know nothing of,
Mad hours, silence, subterfuge
And all the dark expedients of love.

Pick

A room – a space – a living space
Alive between four walls
ceiling and floor.

In the first wall a door
Threshhold of here and now
Darkened by the stranger's shadow
the messenger from outer space
with news, like the star's light,
news-years out of date.

In the second wall a grate
The hearth is the room's heart
But serves also as link
through the secret channel
of its chimney-shaft
with outside winds and rain.

In the third wall a window
telling the seasons
and the time
by day and night
in subtle changes of the light
and dark behind the pane.

The fourth wall is unbroken
by any aperture:
It is the room's backbone.

Four walls alone
are not a room
You need a roof
or ceiling overhead
to make the space
not only weather-proof
but more especially a dwelling-place
instead
of a walled garden or a yard
The roof stands for shelter.

Although it is the upper limit of a living-space
the ceiling is the room's least obvious surface
Out of sight and out of mind
Batty
Backache for the house-wife and for the
          house-decorator.

Lastly, the floor, the solid floor
Our stand
Our stance
Oh Stanza!
giving the room its form
and each of us his place.

In fact more times than not
the floor we tread
is just the ceiling of another room
the upper limit of another space
alive between four walls
ceiling and floor,
in the first wall a door.

Prospice

169

Peter Redgrove   **Tapestry Moths**
                   (*For Vicky Allen*)

I know a curious moth, that haunts old buildings,
A tapestry moth, I saw it at Hardwick Hall,
'More glass than wall' full of great tapestries
     laddering
And bleaching in the white light from long windows.
I saw this moth when inspecting one of the cloth
     pictures
Of a man offering a basket of fresh fruit through a
     portal
To a ghost with other baskets of lobsters and
     pheasants nearby
When I was amazed to see some plumage of one of
     the birds
Suddenly quiver and fly out of the basket
Leaving a bald patch on the tapestry, breaking up as
     it flew away.
A claw shifted. The ghost's nose escaped. I realized

It was the tapestry moths that ate the colours like
     the light
Limping over the hangings, voracious cameras,
And reproduced across their wings the great scenes
     they consumed
Carrying the conceptions of artists away to hang in
     the woods
Or carried off never to be joined again or packed
     into microscopic eggs
Or to flutter like fragments of old arguments through
     the unused kitchens
Settling on pans and wishing they could eat the
     glowing copper

The lamb-faced moth with shining amber wool
     dust-dabbing the pane
Flocks of them shirted with tiny fleece and picture
     wings

170

The same humble mask flaming in the candle or on
the glass bulb
Scorched unwinking, dust-puff, disassembled; a
sudden flash among the hangings
Like a window catching the sun, it is a flock of
moths golden from eating
The gold braid of the dress uniforms, it is the rank
of the family's admirals
Taking wing, they rise

Out of horny amphorae, pliable maggots, wingless
they champ
The meadows of fresh salad, the green glowing
pilasters
Set with flowing pipes and lines like circuits in green
jelly
Later they set in blind moulds all whelked and horny
While the moth-soup inside makes itself lamb-faced
in
The inner theatre with its winged curtains, the
long-dressed
Moth with new blank wings struggling over tapestry,
drenched with its own birth juices

Tapestry enters the owls, the pipistrelles, winged
tapestry
That flies from the Hall in the night to the street
lamps,
The great unpicturing wings of the nightfeeders on
moths
Mute their white cinders . . . and a man,
Selecting a melon from his mellow garden under a
far hill, eats,
Wakes in the night to a dream of one offering fresh
fruit,
Lobsters and pheasants through a green fluted
portal to a ghost.

London Magazine

Vernon Scannell   **Wish You Were Here**

The sun's brass shout is muffled by a wad
Of woolly cloud; this wind has wandered from
An earlier mood, say March.
Its energy has no good humour in it.
It floats a shiftier beach a foot above
The firm original,
Insinuates grit in sandwiches and eyes.

In spite of drifting sand, a muted sun,
We all, in our own ways, apply ourselves
To this, our annual task
Of relaxation or more active pleasure.
A yellow plastic ball bobs out to sea;
Young men with muscles prance
Or pose and touch their bulges pensively.

They do not touch my heart, as children do
Whose serious play is wholly lacking that
Self-consciousness that robs
The body's speech of plausibility.
The children ply their spades with diligence
Or dare the slavering waves.
Unknowingly they mould a memory.

The old are unselfconscious too. The wives
Lie back in deck-chairs, eyes tight-shut against
The wicked wind-blown sand.
Their husbands, bald and bracered, sleep until
The pubs renew their welcome, opening
Their doors like loving arms.
Incontinent and feline seagulls yaup.

And I, who feel I'm neither young nor old
But obsolete, lie on my bed of beach
And feel the sabulous wind
Spreading its thin coarse sheeting over me.
Ambition, hope, desire are cold. I'll stay
For sand to cover me,
Forgotten culture, not worth digging for.

Meridian

Tonight we drive back late from talk and supper
Across miles of unlit roads, flat field and fen,
Towards home; but on the way must make a detour
And rescue you from what, half-laughingly,
We think of as your temporary world –
Some group or other, all outlandishly
Named and rigged up in fancy dress and loud
With adolescent grief. Well, we're too old
For alien caperings like that. The road
Runs towards home and habit, milk and bed.

That unborn child I locked up in neat stanzas
Survives in two or three anthologies,
An effigy sealed off from chance or changes.
Now I arrive near midnight, but too early
To claim you seventeen years afterwards:
A darkened auditorium, lit fitfully
By dizzy crimsons, pulsing and fading blues
Through which electric howls and snarled-out words
Isolate you (though only in my eyes)
Sitting among three hundred sprawling bodies.

Your pale face for a second looms up through
The jerking filters, splatterings of colour
As if spawned by the music, red and blue
Over and over – there, your face again,
Not seeing me, not seeing anything,
Distinct and separate, suddenly plain
Among so many others, strangers. Smoke
Lifts as from a winter field, obscuring
All but your face, consuming, as I look,
That child I gave protective rhetoric.

Not just this place, the tribal lights, the passive
Communion of noise and being young,
Not just the strident music which I give

No more than half an ear to; but the sense
Of drifting out into another plane
Beyond the one I move on, and moved once
To bring you into being – that is why
I falter as I call you by your name,
Claim you, as drifting up towards me now
You smile at me, ready for us to go.

Encounter

David Wright   **Not so much an Elegy**
(i.m. Brian Higgins 1930–1965)

Six months underground at Birstall where he came
from,
Elegies begin to appear in the public prints:
Of dead poets, he knew, elegies are the doom;
Also posthumous, unspendable cash. Higgins

Must have known he could not beat that ironic rap.
I've made as much money as ever I gave him,
Writing his obituaries. His manuscript
Remains are being bought by the British Museum

To be laid up for keeps fifty yards from the pub
Where he worked at bumming drinks or a place to
kip,
Or trying to con a publisher out of five quid.
He was that bloody menace, a pure poet.

His friends were his victims and most of his victims
Were poets – some better, but none as pure as he;
I mean as uncompromising in their vocations.
It is known the god of poets is Mercury

Who is also god of thieves; he was twice covered.
Like a knife through butter he went through the
warty boys;
Not for nothing he called himself the northern
fiddler.
Ask George Barker, Anthony Cronin, Dom Moraes.

But, as I said, the elegies are appearing.
Like Higgins, they are outrageous and odd;
Like truth and Hig they spare no room for
affection –
'He was like life' – and life is partly squalid,

Aberrant, arbitrary, undependable;
His most admired master accused – 'He stole my
ham'
As if it were his thunder, which is probable;
Betrayed into self-betrayal, as I am.

Poetry Nation

Kit Wright   **Elizabeth**

*(In the summer of 1968 thousands of people
turned out at the small stations along the route
to see the train carrying the body of Robert
Kennedy from New York to Arlington Memorial
Cemetery in Washington. In Elizabeth, New
Jersey, three people were pressed forward on to
the line by the crowd and killed by a train coming
the other way – I happened to be travelling up by
the next train in this direction and passed the
bodies. One was of a Negro woman.)*

Up from Philadelphia,
Kennedy on my mind,
Found you waiting in Elizabeth,
Lying there by the line.

Up from Philadelphia,
Wasn't going back,
Saw you, then saw your handbag
Forty yards on up the track.

Saw you under a blanket,
Black legs sticking through,
Thought a lot about Kennedy,
Thought a lot about you

Years later

*Blood on the line, blood on the line,
Elizabeth,*
No end, no end to anything,
Nor any end to death.

No public grief by television,
Weeping all over town,
Nobody locked the train up
That struck the mourners down.

Nobody came to see you,
You weren't lying in state,
They swept you into a siding
And said the trains would be late.

They left you there in the siding
Against an outhouse wall
And the democratic Primaries,
Oh they weren't affected at all,

In no way,

Blood on the line, blood on the line,
Elizabeth,
No end, no end to anything,
Nor any end to death.

Sirhan shot down Kennedy,
A bullet in L.A.,
But the one that broke Elizabeth,
It was coming the other way,

Coming on out of nowhere,
Into nowhere sped,
Blind as time, my darling,
Blind nothing in its head.

Elizabeth, Oh Elizabeth,
I cry your name and place,
But you can't see under a blanket,
You can't see anyone's face,

Crying

Blood on the line, blood on the line,
Elizabeth,
No end, no end to anything,
Nor any end to death.

                                                                    B.B.C. 3

Lives of the Poets

A lecture to the Yeats Society at Sligo, 1973.
*(I have left this lecture exactly as it was delivered, a
mere may-fly some trout might take, and no hook in
it. 1974.)*

I have been trying to solve a conundrum: why
should people like you, who know all there is to be
known about William Butler Yeats, ask me, who
know so little, to talk to you? Certainly, the number
of people who knew Yeats diminishes year by year,
but there are still many of them left. Fewer, no
doubt, remember him as long ago as I do, and per-
haps you have listened to them all in turn at your
meetings in Sligo and call on me merely so that you
can tick my name off the list, without any vain hope
that I might tell you something you did not know
already. I am as ill-fitted for the task as any man
could be. I like to mind my own business, so that I
never have inquired into the lives of the people I
know. I haven't the least idea whether my friends
beat their wives or how they go about the mys-
terious feat of getting enough to live on. I don't
suppose Yeats beat his wife: she was too active, but
if you put me on oath I don't know that I could
swear to it.

As to getting a living, Yeats seemed pretty com-
fortable to a young man as hard up as I was, but he
once told me that he was sixty before he earned
£200 a year by writing. I've remembered that be-
cause it filled me with gloomy and far too accurate
notions about my own future. I don't think it throws
much light on his finances, and it may not even be
true, since men use good round terms when they
advise younger men against writing for a living.
They are engaged in advocacy, not history, and don't
expect to have their summary accounts audited.

I have confessed that I am not curious about other men's lives, so that I haven't much to remember. Now I must add that I don't study to remember, because I have always found Memory to be a cunning and persistent liar, which no doubt explains why the Muses, her daughters, are so unreliable. Whenever accident enables me to check the facts, memory seems to be wrong. If I consider Yeats, as you have obliged me to, I begin to wonder whether God had any hand in the man I remember at all or whether I have created him all by myself. You will understand why I prefer to see poets only through the print on the pages of their collected works, with no intervening memories, not even their own. My shrivelled remains of a conscience reminded me of this before I accepted your invitation to talk about Yeats, but, as I think Shaw said, every man of forty is a scoundrel, and a man as old as I am is more than a match for whatever conscience he has left.

The printed mentions of me that Yeats has left are not at all flattering. In one place – I cannot give you the reference – he shows some alarm at the prospect of meeting one of the wilder disciples of Ezra Pound. At another – *Pages from a Diary*, on the seventh page – he shows himself disturbed by my conversation, though he is also kind enough to say that he had admired my verse. The conversation was about God and the church, and young men are apt to be very summary in their judgements of such matters, and crude in expressing them. I wonder whether Yeats ever discovered that I was a Quaker, if not in intellectual persuasion, at least by temperament and education. However that may be, he got used to me. I witnessed his will – the next passerby would have done as well for that – and I was sent to Switzerland to collect his children from their school and conduct them by easy stages to Rapallo.

It was at Rapallo that I met him. I dined or lunched or supped or underwent some similar formal presentation in the flat he had taken at the top of a big modern block overlooking the bay. I remember nothing about it, but a little later at some similar meeting he astonished me by reciting to his guests the whole twenty-eight lines of one of my poems, word-perfect, though to me, at first, almost unrecognisable in his hieratic chant. I don't know whether this was an extreme case of the common politeness of getting by heart some quotation from the poet you are entertaining and uttering it at the first plausible opportunity, or whether he really liked it. Perhaps he did, for it was written when I was under the spell of Mallarmé and might have sounded like an echo of tunes he had been familiar with in his youth. I don't recollect this out of pride, for Yeats admired and praised some poems I would hate mine to be ranked with, but because it seemed a very handsome amends to make for his initial distrust. From then on he talked freely with me whenever we met.

That was not so often as might be imagined, because Yeats was ill a good deal of the time. He had the disease which was called, in those days, Malta fever, because Maltese were said to catch it from the goats whose milk they drank; but it had been called relapsing fever, a better name, since patients are continually getting better and then suddenly showing all the symptoms again as badly as ever or even worse. At one time Yeats certainly thought that he was dying, and that is why Ezra Pound and I were suddenly called to witness his will. However, he got better again and again and relapsed again and again. At one time he would be strolling about the town – a little town still in those days – and at another he would be what the hospitals now call 'serious'. This went on so long that he began to think he had been bewitched, so that the doctors were helpless: what he needed was a powerful and well-disposed wizard. But for magic he had only himself to rely on in that time and place, and he was often too ill even to think fruitfully about magic. However he did at last convince himself – perhaps I ought to rephrase that – he did at last manage to humbug himself into believing that his illness was caused by a certain ring he wore, and the next time he was strong enough to venture out, he and Mrs Yeats made their way to the end of the mole and cast the ring into the sea, with the appropriate formula; and it seemed to work, for that time he did not relapse, which confirmed him in his half-belief in magic.

Yeats's illness is also connected with the story of the suicidal cat. In those days there lived, in a fantastical villa at Zoagli, near Rapallo, an Italian dramatic poet called Sem Benelli of whom I can say very little except that his work answered well in the theatre, so that he grew rich, ran his own theatre company, and enjoyed the society of extravagant beautiful actresses. His current mistress lay in bed to all hours of the day, caressing an exceedingly fine white Persian cat, until another play was ready for production and Sem Benelli's company had to set out on tour. Then they were puzzled what to do with the cat, till Sem Benelli's secretary, who was a friend of mine, remembered that I was living alone in a flat above Rapallo and might possibly welcome the cat's company, but he was not sure, so he never asked me. He went about things in a less simple style. One day I heard a sort of scuffle on the stairs, and then a knock at my door, which I opened just in time to catch a glimpse of petticoats whirling as some peasant girl ran away. I couldn't chase her, because I tripped over a basket that had been left on the threshold, and the basket mewed. When I opened it and saw the magnificent cat, with its long silky white hair, its pink nose and blue eyes, I couldn't imagine where it had come from or why it had been left at my door, but I was rather pleased than otherwise. I gave it milk, and went out to get fish for it, and the cat made itself at home immediately. The girls from next door came to see me a little oftener because of the cat. But my satisfaction didn't last long. The cat was used to being stroked and petted all day. It would never leave me alone. If I wrote, it came and sat on the paper. If I typed, it tried to sit on the typewriter. Whenever I put it down it complained, and looked so hurt that I had to stop working to comfort it, and thus I grew more and more exasperated and left off considering the cat's feelings. At last one day when I had put it down, it jumped onto the window-sill, called my attention with a prolonged miaow, struck a melodramatic attitude (I assure you) and leapt down three stories into the garden. Perhaps it got rid of one of its nine lives, but in veterinary terms it only dislocated its shoulder. I had that put right, but as soon as the cat was tolerably active again I determined to get rid of it. By that time we had found out where it came from, but Sem Benelli's house was closed and very likely the actress who had fondled the cat had been succeeded by another. I couldn't just return it. I thought of leaving it on somebody's doorstep, as it had been left on mine, but Ezra Pound suggested Yeats. He was ill, too ill to work, but restless, and he might as well fondle the cat; and its attempted suicide was certainly something to ponder on: so the cat was solemnly presented to the great poet and its beauty made it welcome. For a time. Unfortunately – that seems the wrong word – but unfortunately for the cat, Yeats got better and tried to work, but the cat wouldn't let him. While it was with me it had become expert in every means of sabotaging work that a cat is capable of and it toiled with desperation to prevent Yeats thinking of anything whatever except itself. At last it had to be shut out on the balcony, where it leapt onto the balustrade, cut an attitude, proclaimed its intention of suicide, and jumped down, four stories this time, to the pavement. It broke a leg. No one but the vet could take any satisfaction from that, and by now the cat had only seven lives left, so there had to be councils to decide what to do with it. At last it was given to Ezra Pound's father, and there, I believe, it found lasting content, sitting in the sun with that kindest of old men.

I don't know whether Yeats ever alluded to this cat. It seemed just the sort of creature to furnish him with symbols, but I can't remember ever seeing anything I could trace to it. Perhaps, like me, he had a guilty conscience for driving the poor animal to suicide. Anyway, that is the only thing I can tell you about Yeats that is likely to be new to many of you. He strolled sometimes alone along the promenade in a long overcoat and a broad brimmed hat, with his hands often behind him and his eyes on the ground a yard or two in front of his toes, as though the exterior world were as narrow for him as for Wordsworth's Old Cumberland Beggar; the very picture of intent poetic reverie, filling whatever spectators there might be with awe and admiration. But those who got close enough might have seen that his eyes were not fixed on the ground at all. They were darting from side to side, looking for someone to gossip with, and if he spotted an acquaintance – Ezra or George Antheil or me for instance – sitting in the cafe he lost no time in crossing the road to sit with us. You are bound to ask me what his conversation was like and what it was about, and I have to confess that I can't tell you. We enjoyed it, it must have been good conversation, but it had no such marked characteristics as stick in the mind, such as Ezra Pound's lightning and unexpected wit, or the marriage of paradox and commonsense in Shaw, or the belligerence of Wyndham Lewis, or Ford's story-telling. He liked argument so long as it was not too cogent, about religion and the wilder sort of metaphysics – Plotinus, for example. Sometimes he was willing to discuss the technical side of poetry, but on the whole it seemed as though he felt technique to be too intimate a matter for much public discussion. Most of all he loved gossip, current gossip for preference, but old gossip too, as though nothing were ever altogether past and done with. If conversation were in any danger of flagging, you could always revive it by a reference, in any context, to George Moore. Yeats's invective about Moore was always as fresh as though their difference had happened only yesterday. He said he disdained Moore, yet he could never let the subject alone, never dismiss it in weariness, never remember how many years had gone by since Moore's offence.

Fortunately, one of the first pieces of literary work I ever did had been done for George Moore, so that the bait was always at hand and the big fish always rose to it.

Another conversation with Yeats has provided a line for Ezra Pound's *Cantos*. We were sitting inside the cafe on a wet afternoon, eating cakes, George Antheil and I, when Yeats joined us. He must have said something about Shelley, when I, intending to wave a red rag at the bull to liven up the afternoon, announced that there was no good in Shelley whatsoever, except perhaps that he had recommended incest, which, I said, must be the best foundation for domestic tranquillity. Yeats did not bother to come to Shelley's rescue, but began considering my proposition about incest in detail. I forget what he had to say about it, but presently he said: 'Ssshh! If the general public could overhear the conversation of poets, they would hhhang the lot of us'. This was reported to Pound, and it was not wasted on him.

Sometimes he tried to convince me that magic, theosophy, and the rest of his paraphernalia were not just a subjective source of symbols for him, but were real, objective happenings. He gave me some notion of Madame Blavatsky, and her mixture of obvious charlatanry with feats which he thought she really believed, and which he was, provisionally, willing to believe. I had met Annie Besant and been impressed by the force of her personality, but Yeats said she was not to be mentioned in the same breath with Blavatsky. But at this date I could not possibly separate what he said about that formidable woman from what he has written about her, and that you know already. Altogether I think he preferred the wizards of his youth to contemporary wizards. He was not inclined to bother with Gurdjieff, for example, and was uneasy about Aleister Crowley, though eager for all the details of the latest scandal from Crowley's Sicilian den. That kept me in the conversation, because Mary Butts, who had been horrified at Cefalu, had told me all about it when she paused in her flight at Genoa, while it was fresh in her memory and before her memory had had much time to embroider it. There was something about Crowley trying to push somebody over a cliff, though whether the pushing was done physically or by suggestion I'm sure I can't remember now. And something, that Mary didn't like, had happened to a goat, and I hadn't collected enough details about that to satisfy Yeats. Sometimes his pleasure in scandals which must have been terrible to the people concerned rather disgusted me, but this is not the occasion to dwell on that.

In other ways, Yeats was kind and thoughtful of other people. His children possessed a very splendid Wendy-house, but had grown out of it. He handed it over to my little daughter and she and the dog wore it out in a year or two. It must have been troublesome to arrange its transport to Italy. We could never have afforded such an expensive toy. Also he put up with the presence of Antheil or myself at times when he must have found us intrusive, merely because the young learn from the old and the old must let them. Now that I am old myself I realise how much kindness was necessary to show such tolerance.

He had a mint set of the new Irish coinage, with the animals on it, a perquisite of his senatorial labours, and took great pleasure in showing it to us. On the other hand, the Abbey Theatre, his other continuing public activity, did not seem to give him much satisfaction. When Lennox Robinson came to Rapallo to consult him about it, Yeats grew agitated and irritable. I haven't the faintest idea what the trouble was. Perhaps he was just tired of the stage by then.

That, I am afraid, is all I can now remember about Yeats. Of course, there are plenty of general impressions; but they are neither factual nor precise, and I daresay they are derived as much from his writings, and even from other people's talk about Yeats as from genuine memories, accurate or inaccurate. Many of you are probably much better qualified than I am to form such impressions; however, here are some of them, for what they are worth. Some of you probably know better, and some may be annoyed, but I think my impressions are founded on fact, however much they may have strayed in more than forty years.

I am often asked whether Yeats actually believed in magic. 'Belief' is a difficult word, covering everything from immediate conviction, such as comes from what a man sees for himself or similarly immediate experience, to the results of self-hypnosis. Yeats was interested in any evidence he could find for a world that goes beyond the matter science can investigate. He knew by experience that a great deal of what is alleged to be such evidence turns out to be deliberate fraud, but could not give up hoping to find evidence that could not be contradicted. I think he kidded himself that he had found such evidence, and I think he was more than half aware that he was kidding himself. Magic, Rosicrucianism, theosophy, even plain free-masonry, provided him with symbols he could use to build poems with, symbols which had not been overworked by generations of previous poets, which were harder for imitators to acquire than the Irish mythology of his youth, and which could be made to mean almost anything he chose or to mean half a dozen things at once. It was too handy a store to be sacrificed to scepticism. Yet I think scepticism was there underneath. He talked about his theory of the mask: if you wear a mask long enough your own features come to resemble the mask, till it is hardly possible to know for sure whether you are wearing it or not. I think that was his frame of mind about magic. He had made a habit of it which was useful both for writing poetry and for escaping from the materialism of socialists and capitalists, and he felt that if he investigated the origins of his habit too closely he might lose those advantages. A great many people who have what they call religious beliefs have no firmer foundation for their faith than Yeats had for his magic; but their faith is not that of the mystics who have seen God nor the philosophers who have invented him. In most cases I think it is merely self-indulgence, and in others, as with Yeats, a utility, a means to perfectly human ends.

About 1930 I had gone to Siena to look at pictures and stumbled quite unexpectedly on the writings of St Catherine of that city. That very hardheaded and formidable lady drew no line whatever between her dealings with unsatisfactory popes and emperors and her dealings with God. Indeed, she was as tart with one as with the other. Writing political letters and holding the Infant Jesus in her arms were all in the days work for her. It is impossible to know what she meant, but impossible to doubt that *she* knew, quite clearly. God was as much a part of her daily life as dishwashing, and just as concrete and real to her. I was, and still am, greatly impressed. But St

Catherine didn't impress Yeats. His mysticism was not of that kind. His God was not real, but an escape from reality. He was impatient of discussing St Catherine, as he was impatient of discussing George Fox's very immediate dealings with God. Compared with these, Yeats's mysticism was trivial. If he believed it at all, he believed it for his own ends; he sought it, it was not forced upon him.

Magic is primarily a means of exerting power or persuading yourself that you can. Would you rather win the football pools or be granted the cloak of invisibility? Yeats's magic was never as crude as that, but there was something of that sort in it, beyond the help it gave him in writing poetry and the means it gave him of evading materialism. I don't know whether he ever suspected that this third motive might have something to do with his cultivation of theosophy, of Plotinus, and of other anti-rational shortcuts to power. Faustus was damned, mainly, I suppose, for his vulgarity, and Yeats hated vulgarity too much to suspect that a trace of it might linger somewhere in his unconscious motivation. Yet love of power underlies a great deal that is not even superficially mystical in his poetry. He thought of himself as one of a governing class, with obligations, but with privileges too. Disdain of shop-keepers, readiness to snub stone-breakers with political opinions, contempt for the mob, even when the mob was an abstraction, show clearly enough that Yeats felt he had a right to power that he did not share with the greater part of mankind. If you have none of the real power of armies and police and huge fortunes, magic is an unsatisfactory, but often irresistible way of pretending to yourself that you have an equivalent.

Perhaps by now you think that I have forgotten that we are discussing a great poet. Yes, but you have asked me to discuss the man I knew, rather than his poetry. Yes, again, but it is now generally admitted that Yeats was a great poet, nobody needs convincing of that. Rather, it is time to begin considering what his limitations were, so that we can, sooner or later, consign him to his place in the succession of great poets in our language. The young are getting impatient of him, as when I was young we had got impatient of Tennyson or of Swinburne. The young are apt to say that Yeats was an old square, or even a fascist beast. Such criticism may be irrelevant to poetry – I think it is – but it is as well to get it out of the way if possible. There were plenty of other fascist beasts about in the thirties, and among the poets, Yeats's close friend Ezra Pound is the most obvious. Eliot is another, the more insidious for being disguised as an English gentleman. What these poets and many other writers really had in common was a love of order. With order in society it matters little whether you are rich or poor, you will not be harassed by perpetual changes of fortune, you can plan your life's work within known limits, not felt as limits because they are as unavoidable as the limits imposed by our physique or the duration of human life. Whether an orderly society ever really existed or could exist is beside the point. Plato planned one, in our own day the socialists have proposed half a dozen different models for one, and in Yeats's youth William Morris had imagined yet another Utopia and made a great impression with *News from Nowhere*. Yeats went further than the rest when he called for ceremony, manners as elaborate as those he imagined in the Byzantine court. All such fancies assume tacitly that the regulations and ceremonies are made by extremely wise and perfectly unselfish rulers, not by Stalin or Hitler or even Mussolini, and none of their proponents, not Plato himself, pauses to consider where and how such rulers are to be found. The maxims given to guide the wise rulers are plausible and disastrous. You are told how blessed the ruler is who will make two blades of grass grow where one grew before, but never reminded that the people may not give a damn about blades of grass. They may, like the Arabs in Libya and in Palestine, prefer a desert, and there may be good reasons for preferring a desert. Abdulaziz Ibn Saud might have listed them. The blades of grass maxim is the standard excuse for imperialism, and I think Yeats would never have used it; but it lurks under all utopian dreams of order.

Weighing this up, if it is worth weighing at all, you must of course allow for my own conviction that 'God is the dividing sword', and that order is no more than a rather unfortunate accident that sometimes hampers civilization. But my purpose is only to remind some critics that Yeats's love of order is something he shared with Dante and Shakespeare and probably far more than half of the world's great poets, as well as with nearly all the philosophers and historians. His way of expressing it was his own; he took his instances largely from the world around him, that of the Anglo-Irish gentry, which differs in personnel from the hierarchy of the church or of business management or of the civil service, but does not differ from them in principle. He was much nearer to Bernard Shaw than he would have liked to think.

Still, if Yeats's political thought hardly differed at bottom from what was current all around him, if his philosophic, theosophic, magical quasi-religion was trivial and by origin insincere, politics and religion were not his business except in the sense in which they are everyone's business. He was a poet. It is true that he loaded his conception of being a poet with all manner of lofty moral responsibilities, which seemed to claim authority in politics and religion. He wrapped an invisible bardic cloak around him whenever he uttered a line of anyone's verse. His determination that poetry should be noble rather starved his own of the humour which was part of his conversation. But for him, at least in middle-age, poetry needed no formal thought, no logical theory. It was in him. Just as we say some painter thinks with his brush, so Yeats thought with his pen, and if his pen ever misled him on purely poetical matters, it was so rarely that I cannot think of an instance, though perhaps a search through his volume might bring a few to light. I don't suppose that he was born that way. So far as my experience goes, poetry is a craft hard to learn and only acquired by long apprenticeship. In these days, of course, there is no one for a man to be apprenticed to except himself, so that diligence is more necessary than ever. Yeats was diligent. He must have taught his ear to attend to rhythm and vowel sequence and what the Welsh have codified but the rest of us grope for to hold the sounds of our verse together; yet he learnt all these so early that people who are content with inaccurate phrases would say he was born with them.

What did he read? What lines echoed in his mind? Perhaps some of you know. I don't. I only see that already in 1889 *The Wanderings of Oisin* gave notice to those who had ears to hear that a great poet had arisen in Ireland. It is a young man's work, not quite autonomous. There is a surrender to sound which must owe something to Swinburne, and, through Swinburne, you can hear now and then a hint of Tennyson's trickiness. There is an evident intention to vie with the swift course of William Morris's best work, and some miscalculation in this, for Morris's had, in, say, *The Defence of Guenevere*, matter enough to keep the poem tearing along at a great pace, but the story Yeats had chosen is short of incidents. It would languish if he did not keep it alive by tricks of sound. All this granted, Oisin is still a poem that holds its readers, and here and there in it are lines which go so straight to their point that neither Tennyson nor Swinburne could ever have written the like. I don't mean a logical point, nor even a narrative point, but lines which convey an entire atmosphere in four or five words, or set the pace of a whole episode. There are vivid lines that contrast with the dreamlike confusion of other passages, and make the dream endurable that would bore us but for these interruptions of its mistiness. The onomatopeic skills of Oisin are as well worth investigating as the symbolic intricacies of Byzantium.

Agenda

He was old when we met him first, the grizzled veteran of a thousand wars, literary and other, and standing then on the brink of his eightieth birthday. They said that he would celebrate the occasion quietly in Paris, taking the train from Mestre in a day or two. This was thought to be fitting for several reasons, not least that Paris was the place where he had established himself forty years earlier as both catalyst and contributor to modern literature – a bearded Caliban, in his own words, fiercely intent upon casting out the Ariel of pretentious rhetoric.

The idea of meeting him had come up casually enough the night before. We were dining on scampi and grilled tournedos in Harry's Bar, enriched by small glasses of champagne in a seemingly endless procession. Young Cipriani, the manager's son, hovered attentively. He was an old friend of our host, Gianfranco Ivancich – handsome, brown-haired, brown-eyed, forty-five, kindly, generous, brilliant, and articulate, a Venetian by ancient lineage. Some said his family could have belonged to the Italian nobility, though they had long ago declined the honor.

'Do you know Pound, Ezra Pound?' Gianfranco said.

'No. Is he here?'

'In Venice, yes. Across the Canal.' Gianfranco pointed over his shoulder. 'Have you met him?'

'No. Only an exchange of letters, not very satisfactory.'

'Recently?'

'Six or seven years ago.'

'You did not quarrel?'

'Not exactly.'

'I am giving him lunch tomorrow. He will soon be

eighty. He is leaving for Paris the day after. Will you come?'

'Yes,' we said, and it was arranged.

Next morning Gianfranco appeared promptly at our hotel, still merry and bright and full of talk. We crossed a corner of the Piazza San Marco and boarded the traghetto. The day was bright and cool, with a brisk breeze. 'Ideal October,' said Gianfranco, gazing back at the Palace of the Doges. Waves were slapping the docks of the line of hotels. The far side was sunnier and warmer. Our feet echoed on the pavements and made small thunder-sounds over the arches of the lesser bridges. Deep in the warren of dwellings and shops we crossed a final canal. Gianfranco pointed out the house of Cipriani. 'It is where he stores the wines for Harry's Bar,' he said, 'and here is Mr. Pound's.'

It was a narrow house fronting the sidewalk. The handsome white-haired lady who answered our knock was Olga Rudge, an Ohioan by birth, a former concert violinist, the mother of Pound's daughter Mary. She embraced Gianfranco, shook our hands. The ground-floor room was square and rather barely furnished, with an open fireplace and a narrow stairway leading to the room above, the twin of this one. An American girl was there also, very pleasant and quick, with a short neat haircut. Last year she had done a portrait head of Pound, cast now in bronze. Neither the head nor the poet was yet visible.

He came deliberately down the stairs, a tall old man with square shoulders and thinning hair abundantly long and swept back from his forehead. Both beard and hair were gray, not white. His eyes were blue and he had a way of opening them wide and fixing his visitors with an intense stare, all the more disconcerting because the stare was not accompanied by speech. He was meticulously clean – hair, skin, the knobbly hands, the nails – and as gracious as one can be without words. The suit he wore was of gray flannel, with a blue shirt and a dark blue Italian tie. He shook his head vigorously when Miss Rudge insisted that he wear a topcoat but in the end, as we walked out, he made a compromise, draping the camel's hair coat like a cloak around his shoulders, and carrying a cane of yellow wood. 'He must always have his stick,' said Olga Rudge, smiling.

We had heard of his decrepitude, but it did not show. His carriage was erect, his gait deliberate and easy, there was neither hesitation nor shuffling as he picked up his black shoes rhythmically and set them firmly down. When I walked ahead to snap his picture as he crossed a couple of bridges, he turned profile at the moment the shutter clicked. He was very slender, probably weighing no more than a hundred and twenty-five, and in profile rather hawk-like. His head was thrown back, he was enjoying the sun and the light breeze. A few Venetians greeted him as he passed and he bowed back politely, with never a break in his stride. He might have been a lord.

This meeting, I thought, was like coming into a strange theater towards the end of the final act. We knew in a general way the drift the play had taken: the birth-scene far off in Hailey, Idaho, in 1885; the bachelor and master of arts in 1905–1906; the expatriate on the grand tour in 1907. We had read the early books, 'A Lume Spento', and then those others that came in quick succession after he had settled in England, 'Personae', 'Exultations', 'Canzoni', 'Ripostes'. The learned and multilingual young man established a reputation so rapidly that Robert Frost, meeting him in London in 1913, could write home to a friend, 'I don't mind his calling me raw. He is reckoned raw himself and at the same time perhaps the most prominent of the younger poets here.' W. B. Yeats praised his 'vigorous creative mind', adding that he was 'certainly a creative personality of some sort', even though it was still too early to predict his future line of development. 'His experiments are perhaps errors', wrote Yeats, 'but I would always sooner give the laurel to vigorous errors than to any orthodoxy not inspired'. And then later at Stone Cottage, Coleman's Hatch, in Sussex, while the war raged across the Channel: 'Ezra Pound and his wife are staying with me, we have four rooms of a cottage on the edge of a heath and our back is to the woods.'

It was Yeats who had told Pound that Frost's 'North of Boston' was the best thing that had come out of America for some time. Frost, rather bemusedly, called Pound 'the stormy petrel' who had sent a 'fierce article' to Harriet Monroe's Poetry magazine in Chicago, 'denouncing a country that neglects fellows like me.' Yet Frost, though glad enough of the public acclaim, could not help feeling that Pound was concerned with personal power. 'All I asked', he wrote, in a free-verse poem addressed to Pound but wisely never sent, 'was that you should hold to one thing: that you considered me a poet. That was why I clung to you as one clings to a group of insincere friends for fear they shall turn their thoughts against him the moment he is out of hearing. The truth is I was afraid of you'.

Others feared him, too, but turned to him for aid. Helping to launch and publicize the Imagist movement, guiding such little magazines as The Egoist, Blast, and The Little Review, he had hurled himself with restless energy into a program for the rehabilitation of modern poetry, backed by what Harriet Monroe called his 'love of stirring up and leading forth other minds'. T. S. Eliot soon acknowledged his priceless editorial assistance with 'The Waste Land' by dedicating the poem to him and lauding him in Dante's phrase as 'il miglior fabbro', as, in a manner of speaking, he had turned out to be. Ernest Hemingway, on first meeting him in Paris in 1922, had written, like Frost before him, an attack on Pound that was never sent, though presently, as he told a friend, he discovered that Pound was really 'a great guy and a wonderful editor', and volunteered to teach Ezra to box in return for lessons in how to write.

Some years later, when Hemingway gashed his forehead in a domestic accident, Pound sent him from Rapallo a typical message: 'Haow the hell-sufferin tomcats did you git drunk enough to fall upwards thru the blithering skylight!!!!' And Hemingway, four years after that, stated forthrightly that 'any poet born in this century or in the last ten years of the preceding century who can honestly say that he has not been influenced by or learned greatly from the work of Ezra Pound deserves to be pitied rather than rebuked.'

So we came that noonday in Venice by tortuous route to the door of the small ristorante where Gianfranco was known and received with obvious affection, and where Pound was treated with the deference due his age and reputation. He sat down at one end of the table and Gianfranco, flanked by Olga Rudge and the girl sculptress, at the other. Pound listened intently to all that was said, nodded and smiled in response to observations, widened his eyes once or twice in that special gesture of his, and said absolutely nothing. Gianfranco had warned us of this 'vow of silence', and thought that it was an act of contrition for having said too much over Rome Radio in the time of Mussolini. At home, of course, he talked with those closest to him, to his beautiful daughter Mary at Schloss Brunnenburg, to his adoring grandchildren. The taciturnity was reserved for public gatherings, and this counted as one. As befitted his years, he ate sparely, declining soup and only lightly sampling the *malfatta*, a delicious kind of ravioli cut on the bias. After two mouthfuls he pushed his plate away, astonishing my wife by saying to her the only two words he had yet uttered: 'too heavy'. At the next course he delicately made way with two small scallopini washed down with half a glass of dry white wine.

I mentioned the letter he had sent me from Rapallo in the spring of 1959, less than a year after his release from twelve years' imprisonment in St. Elizabeths Hospital in Washington, D.C. It was a typically aggressive and humorous-serious document poorly typed with blue ribbon on stationery of the Albergo Grande Italia & Lido, and dated April seventh.

Carlos Baker, Princeton, where Woodrow slopped. Yr/ bk/ on Hem, serious re/ literature and Paris, but you are ham ignorant of history. Whether any servant of Princeton dares combat the age-old falsification and READ any history, let alone adjusting his ideas to the 17 facts that the sons of hell and brain-washed adorers of F. D. R. spend billions to hide I do not know. There are faint signs that soon truth will trickle into the margins, but not into the main stream of u.s. university sewage. I see Chris Gauss [Dean of the College at Princeton who had died in November, 1951] has passed on, but suppose Dex. White still rates above Andrew in Niebuhrian rhomboids.

frankly yrs. Ez Pound.

At this date I could not recall enough of the letter to quote back at its author, but I did speak of Christian Gauss, at which Pound nodded and smiled, and I wondered aloud at what he had meant by the phrase 'Niebuhrian rhomboids'. But Pound only grinned, folding his thin clean hands on the table before him.

The voluble conversation at the other end of the table now drew us in. We knew only vaguely of Pound's happy liaison of many years with Olga

Rudge, and of their child, Mary de Rachewiltz, now a beautiful woman of forty who lived with her half-Russian, half-Italian husband in a castle in the Tyrol. It was not in fact until six years later, with the publication of Mary's charming autobiography, that we learned the whole romantic story. The book was called 'Discretions' as a kind of echo of her father's 'Indiscretions', published in 1923 only a couple of years before Mary was born at Bressanone. At the time of her birth another woman in the maternity ward had lost her baby and it was arranged that she should nurse the skinny little girl to blooming health, which she achieved in the farming community of Gais in the Tyrol as fosterchild to Johanna Marcher. The Marchers she called Mamme and Tatte. Pound and Olga Rudge were known to her as Mammile and Tattile, although later she began to call Pound by the name of Babbo, and went often to Venice so that her real parents could smooth away the rough edges of her peasant upbringing; here she learned Italian and English as supplementary to the Tyrolese patois that she spoke the rest of the year, swam at the Lido under Babbo's admiring supervision, and was hopefully given a violin by her gifted mother. Educated at a convent school in Florence with the musical name of Regio Instituto delle Nobili Signore Montalva alla Quiete, she first went to Rapallo just before the war, and fell in love with Casa 60, Sant' Ambrogio, a tall house of orange stucco with painted Ionic columns and a green front door overgrown with honeysuckle. She was back in Gais when the news filtered through that Italy had surrendered, and she worked steadily through the rest of the war in hospitals in the north of Italy while Babbo kept quietly at his translations.

Then in 1945 a pair of partisans, ex-fascist convicts eager for reward money, knocked with the butt of a gun on the door at Sant' Ambrogio. Babbo was working on Confucius. 'Seguici, traditore', they said, and took him away. Olga Rudge and Mary saw him later at the Disciplinary Training Center near Pisa. He had aged noticeably; the army fatigues he was wearing did not fit his slender frame; he was writing the first batch of Pisan Cantos on a borrowed typewriter. When Mary saw him in 1953, he had already languished for eight years in the Washington madhouse under indictment for treason. She must not bring her children there, he told her. 'St. Elizabeths is no fit place for the children to see their grandfather in. And there are rumors: granpaw might get sprung.' Then one evening she heard the Italian newscast: il poeta Americano had been released, the indictment dismissed. After twelve years in limbo he could return to Italy on board the *Cristoforo Colombo*, a voyage of discovery in reverse. In Sirmione in 1957 Mary had said to Archibald MacLeish, who had labored so long to set Pound free, 'He has a right to do whatever he likes, anything that makes him happy. . . .' After his release MacLeish sent a generous check to be used to keep Pound warm and there was another from Hemingway that he framed as a memento of an old friendship.

If his remorse still held, it did not show as he sat happily in this small left-bank ristorante. Except for the silences in the intervals of the conversation. Afterwards we ambled back to the narrow little house beside the small canal where a green bottle, some bits of straw, and a hemisphere of orange peel floated somnolently. Pound climbed the steps slowly to the skylighted room at the top of the house. He was not puffing and his color was good, though in that severe light his face looked drawn and the skin almost transparent. He drank a demitasse and took a sip or two of brandy. When a tape recording of a recent canto was put on and played, he listened attentively to his own voice, reading the lines with a kind of gruff eloquence and pronouncing the frequent foreign phrases with the easy skill of an old European hand. When we left he stayed in his chair, watching the patterns of afternoon sunlight on the floor.

Two afternoons later in Paris, Pound and Miss Rudge were met by Dominique de Roux, who was then on the point of publishing the first French translation of the 'Cantos'. 'He is in a state of profound remorse,' M. de Roux told reporters. The vow of silence was still in effect, though he relented occasionally. 'I regret my past errors,' he told de Roux, 'but I hope to have done a little something for some artists.'

On Friday the 29th, the day before his birthday, he sat on a sofa beside Miss Natalie Barney in the drawing room of her house where she had entertained the Parisian intellectuals of the 1920's and wordlessly received old friends and new admirers. He wore horn-rimmed glasses, a checked brown sports jacket, brown pants, and crepe-soled shoes. The long wings of his shirt collar were spread as of old over his lapels, and his hands rested on the grip of his yellow cane. Asked who were his favorite modern poets, he named Cummings and Auden, and permitted himself a two-word judgment of the work of Allen Ginsberg. 'He's vigorous,' said Pound. It was the word Yeats had used for Pound's own talent long ago in England.

By this date we were far away among the Austrian Alps, staying at the Hotel Taube in the market village of Schruns in the Vorarlberg. While Babbo sat beside Miss Barney on the Parisian sofa, we were walking out to the neighboring village of St. Gallenkirch. Some of the men of the town were laying sewer-pipe along the bank of the stream, and others were raking leaves. Bedding was being aired at the windows of the houses, and some of the women were sweeping their porches with rough brooms made of twigs. The lunch at the Taube was typical –

four small trout apiece, cooked whole, with a home-made champignon soup, parsleyed potatoes, and a salad of lettuce, red peppers, white beans, string beans, and cole slaw. For dessert there were rolled pancakes with a custard filling.

After one bite, my wife pushed her dessert-plate towards me across the table.

'Don't you like them?'

'Yes, but after all the rest, they're too heavy.'

'You're echoing Ezra Pound.'

'Yes,' she said. 'Poor old man.'

The Virginia Quarterly Review

The story of my growing-up in poetry is largely connected with the history of the Group, once upon a time highly controversial, and now, I notice, on the verge of becoming 'historic', like one of those second-rate Victorian country houses the impoverished owners throw open to visitors, in imitation of Woburn and Chatsworth.

I was not its founder. That honour belongs to Philip Hobsbaum. Philip had been an undergraduate at Cambridge, reading English at Downing, while I was studying history at Oxford. He saw one of my poems in an undergraduate magazine, liked it, and wrote to me about it. This was a very special kind of honour, and I was appropriately flattered. We Oxford poets had an inferiority complex about our Cambridge contemporaries. The chief cause was Thom Gunn. Though his first collection, *Fighting Terms*, did not appear until 1954, the poems he was publishing in magazines were already much discussed, and were causing ripples in a literary world well beyond our own student environment.

It is not difficult to explain the immediate success that Gunn's early poems enjoyed. A Cambridge passion for Eng. Lit. was combined with a rather taking bully-boy strut; aggressive phrases and rhythms strained, but never broke, the boundaries of conventional forms:

> *Hacks in the fleet and nobles in the Tower.*
> *Shakespeare must keep the peace, and Johnson's*
>   *thumb*
> *Be branded (for manslaughter), in the power*
> *Of irons lay the admired Southampton.*
> *Above all swayed the diseased and doubtful queen:*
> *Her state canopied by the glamour of pain.*

In the circumstances of the time, it was a heady mixture. In Gunn's work, the meritocrats found a new day-dream – that of the academic as man of action.

However, it turned out that Philip was not an admirer of Gunn's. He was eager to introduce me to the work of two Cambridge poets whose work I had not as yet heard of: Ted Hughes and Peter Redgrove. But, more important than this, he was hoping to put into practice an idea he had derived from working with Dr. Leavis.

This emerged when at last we met each other – I think I had not as yet left the R.A.F., but was just about to obtain my discharge. He told me that he was planning to run a series of literary evenings at his flat near Marble Arch, and asked me to come along to them.

Philip's plan was very simple. He planned to base himself on Dr. Leavis's teaching methods, but to apply these to the work of his contemporaries. A text would be put in front of us, and we would be asked to react to it, and to discuss it as candidly as we liked. In addition to the fact that the work would be new, with nothing known about it from previous reports or experience, there would be another significant deviation from university practice. The discussion group would be a complete democracy. The moderator would undertake a purely technical function – that of keeping the discussion going on reasonably coherent lines – but there would be no question of him putting himself above the rest.

The plan worked, rather to my surprise. Though the early meetings of the group were disorderly, in comparison to the more typical sessions which came later, those of us who came regularly found that we were becoming deeply involved in these weekly gatherings, and that surprisingly much came out of them. Most of the credit belonged to Philip. He had a number of qualities, some intellectual, and some physical, which made him a good chairman. He was fond of argument in the way that other men are fond of food. He got enormous enjoyment from its twists and turns, while at the same time he had no patience with slipshod thinking or intellectual evasiveness. The fact that he had, at that time, no poetic ambitions himself, but intended to concentrate on writing novels, made him acceptable to the rest of us. Often he seemed impatient, and inclined to hector and browbeat, and the disputes would often grow noisy and acrimonious. But the forcefulness of his manner concealed a respect for intellectual democracy which he carried very far. He said, and really seemed to believe, that almost anyone had it in them to write a good poem, if only they could be persuaded to ask themselves the right questions. For a long time I too tried to make this proposition an article of faith. The fact that I can no longer do so argues, perhaps, for a loss of confidence in the possibilities offered by poetry, rather than for a loss of confidence in human nature. Finally, there was the fact that Philip was a marvellous reader, with an exceptionally beautiful voice. In the course of a discussion he would lavish prodigies of skill on an apparently feeble and hopeless text; and it was these readings which often persuaded us to look again at something we had felt inclined to dismiss out of hand.

Gradually, during its first year of operation, the discussion group evolved an agreed method of operation. For example, each meeting would be devoted to the work of one writer, as this seemed to provide a much greater continuity of discussion. And, since the work was to be cyclo-styled, so that everyone could have a copy of the text in his or her hand, then it seemed better to have it ready the week beforehand. Those who came to a particular meeting could take next week's sheet away with them. To the others, it would be sent by post. Gradually the mailing-list grew, until the 'songsheets', as they were called, achieved the status of an informal (and free) poetry magazine. But this was a long time later.

The composition of the discussion group itself was very various. Philip brought in his university crony Peter Redgrove, whose work he greatly admired – and there were readings, in the early days, of poems Ted Hughes sent over from America, where he was then teaching. Peter and Ted had both attended similar, but less ambitious, readings organized by Philip at Cambridge. Yet another recruit from Cambridge was the Canadian poet, David Wevill, whose poems shared an expressionist character with those of Hughes and Redgrove.

Meanwhile, I brought in some of the poets I had known at Oxford, notably George MacBeth and Alan Brownjohn. But, despite the fact that the meetings had been started on the basis of university experience, and despite the number of recent Oxbridge graduates who came to them, the Group (for it now seems reasonable to award it a capital letter) soon took on an anti-academic tinge. Some of the most important of the members had not been to either Oxford or Cambridge, and a few had no university education at all. Martin Bell, older than the rest of us, had read English at University College, Southampton, and had then served in the Royal Engineers throughout the war. He was now working as a teacher. A chance meeting with Redgrove (they lived in the same suburb) had brought him back to poetry, after many years of not writing verse. Another important recruit was a young Australian, Peter Porter, then working as an assistant in an Oxford Street bookshop.

One striking feature of the Group, especially if one looks at the list of poets whose work is included in *A Group Anthology* – this, published in 1963, represents a rather later stage in our evolution – is the large number of members who were born abroad.

In addition to a Canadian, an Australian and a Jamaican (myself), there are Taner Baybars, who is a Cypriot Turk, and the Pakistani writer Zulfikhar Ghose. Another oddity of the Group's composition, less easily detectable until one had met the bulk of the regular membership, was that few of the leading lights had done National Service. Some had been exempted on medical grounds – Hobsbaum himself, for example, suffered from very poor eyesight – and some had not been liable because of their Commonwealth citizenship.

It was factors such as these which helped to mould the Group into something more than the sum of its parts. As the weekly meeting continued – they were soon moved to a flat Philip and his wife rented in a strange, leafy enclave in Stockwell – the Group became a living entity, with a character of its own. In part, that character reflected the times. In part, it was an expression of our separate personalities and backgrounds, and of the way in which these reacted upon and modified each other. And in part it grew from the methods we used.

The late fifties were a period of rumbling discontent among intellectuals. Their disaffection made a sharp contrast to the prosperous complacency of the rest of the country. The impact which this outburst of intellectual protest had upon us was modified by our own personal circumstances. I have mentioned, for instance, that when I came to London I got a job in an advertising agency. Redgrove was also in advertising – his father was prominent in the profession. Later, Peter Porter was to leave his bookshop and become a copywriter. At one time, he, Redgrove and I all worked for the same firm.

Advertising was one of the great bugbears of the new rebels – they blamed it for the corruption and the complacency of the society they wanted to scrap. For them, it was a cause, not a symptom. We, making a modest living by it, were inclined to take the opposite view. When the Group became both well-known and unpopular (as we shall see, it had a success which aroused a great deal of jealousy), this connection with advertising was one of the reproaches which was most regularly flung at our heads. We were, all of us, 'copywriter poets', just as the poets group under the banner of the Movement could never shake off the label 'academic'.

What advertising experience did was to make us acknowledge, not only the appetites and the customs, but the characteristic imagery of the urban society that surrounded us. This was most conspicuously true of the work of Peter Porter. Porter, when he first read to the Group, had been one of those young poets who are the despair of critics because they write in an elliptical private language, too confident of their own intelligence to state the obvious. He, blinking at us through his horn-rimmed glasses, was taken aback by our vehement refusal to understand phrases and sentences which seemed to him perfectly clear. But gradually his work came into focus:

This new Daks suit, greeny-brown,
Oyster coloured buttons, single vent, tapered
Trousers, no waistcoat, hairy tweed – my own:
A suit to show responsibility, to show
Return to life – easily got for two pounds down
Paid off in six months – the first stage of the
    change.
I am only the image I can force upon the town.

The 'coming into focus' was, of course, a twofold process. The poet became less cryptic; the audience learned to stretch their own capacities, in order to absorb the new things he was trying to say.

Our mutual bias was, in any case, not only towards clarity, but toward concreteness. Looking at *A Group Anthology* now, I am struck, to use an art critic's term, by the naturalism of its contents. This tendency was made the more emphatic by the fact that many of us soon started to experiment with the dramatic monologue. The reason for this was the circumstances in which we found ourselves. The Group provided every poet who attended it with an audience he could envisage – not solitary readers unknown to him, not a sea of faces in a vague 'cut there' but a roomful of people with familiar personalities. Using the dramatic monologue was a way of speaking out, and yet of preserving a screen between oneself and these friends whom one knew perhaps too intimately. Reading poems aloud encouraged the use of colloquial language, and the deliberate creation or some character of personality, separate from oneself, as a vehicle for what one wanted to say.

Oddly enough, we arrived at the dramatic monologue before we came to Browning. But what we were doing did suggest, at least to me, that Browning would be a good poet to look at. Some of the long poems I wrote at a time when the Group was fully established – monologues put into the mouths of painters such as Rubens and Caravaggio – were undoubtedly the most Browningesque products of our joint enterprise. Yet it was also a reading of Browning which suggested to me the first doubts about what we were doing. The inclusiveness of the great Victorians contrasted with our own exclusiveness, particularly in regard to any poetry not written in English.

Of course, a little influence filtered in from French – Redgrove made some variations on Rimbaud's prose-poems, which seemed to attract him chiefly because of the violence of their imagery, Martin Bell wrote transpositions of Laforgue, Alan Brownjohn's adaptation of a poem by Prevert, 'We are going to see the rabbit', appears in *A Group Anthology*. But none of this showed any real curiosity about what French poets might be writing contemporaneously with ourselves. The Group played no real part in the birth of the translation movement which flourished in the sixties, though a number of individual Group poets followed in its wake.

Something ought also to be said about the political isolation of the Group. Since it was founded and flourished just in the days when the New Left was at its height, and when CND polarized the emotions and the energy of many writers (the first Aldermaston March took place at Easter 1958), one might have expected to find a political overtone in our discussions. One might also have thought that many directly political poems would be read at our evenings. This was not the case. A poem like Alan Brownjohn's 'William Empson at Aldermaston' was the exception rather than the rule.

What did flavour our poetry was a general sense of the terror of the times. It emerged most strongly, perhaps, in some of Redgrove's fantasies, and in the poetry of MacBeth and Porter. Porter's work was often leavened with a sardonic humour which made it memorable:

> *London is full of chickens on electric spits,*
> *Cooking in windows where the public pass.*
> *This, say the chickens, is their Auschwitz,*
> *And all poetry eaters are psychopaths.*

MacBeth's horrors, more often than not, had a *grand guignol* element which made it hard to be certain how seriously he meant them to be taken.

I have wondered, since, if the ambiguity of MacBeth's writing, now latent, now overt, wasn't his form of defence to the psychic pressures which the Group put on all of us. In those days, 'group therapy' wasn't the fashionable concept it has now become; and my feeling is that we were remarkably innocent about psychology, and not especially interested in it. Yet it was inevitable that a discussion of the faults to be found in the poem should touch, at least by implication, on the flaws to be found in the person. The great emphasis we put, largely thanks to Philip, on both clarity of intention as well as clarity of expression, often led us towards dangerous areas. Since the poem itself had often been written to purge or reconcile some conflict it could sometimes only be criticized by pointing out that the purgation was incomplete, or that the battle was being fought on the wrong ground. A discussion might sometimes become a collective effort, on the part of the rest of us, to force the poet whose work was under discussion that night to acknowledge some characteristic which we all saw in him, and which he was determined to deny. Such discussions required skill on the part of the moderator if they were not to become personal slanging matches. They also required, and still more urgently, a mutual trustfulness. When I look back on the Group, I think this is the aspect of it which I remember with the greatest nostalgia. In some curious way we really did manage to trust one another not to use the information which the poems and discussions provided in ways which might be hurtful. If one considers the vanity and egotism of young writers – and few of us were exempt – this candour was surprising.

Since the Group lasted for such a long period – it flourished for ten years, first under Philip's chairmanship and then under mine, it would be surprising if one did not recall disadvantages and flaws, as well as what was good about it. Of all the disadvantages, the most crucial, and perhaps the least expected by us when we began – but then we were all idealists – turned out to be the inflexibility of the personalities involved. After some years of regular meetings, it was possible to anticipate nearly all the arguments which would be produced for or against a particular poem, and sometimes, even, the very phrases which would be uttered in the course of the discussion.

For the newcomer, who heard his poems discussed for the first time, the procedure remained fascinating. Even if the verdict was unfavourable, a young poet found it flattering to be the focus of such concentrated attention, on the part of men who were, by this time, extremely fluent controversialists. For the old hands, I suspect, the discussions grew gradually, and perhaps imperceptibly, less valuable. All too often I found that I was listening, not to the argument itself, but to the undercurrent, seeking a hint of a reaction which was unexpected or not according to rule. In the final years of my chairmanship, I took a lot of trouble to seek out recruits who, I hoped, would rebel against the prevailing orthodoxies. All too often, I would be drawn aside at the end of the evening, and asked why I had invited 'that dreadful man', who was so clearly out of sympathy with everything we stood for.

As one might expect, the Group was not the only thing of its kind which flourished in London at that period. A number of us also went to the gatherings which G. S. Fraser, who had now left the *New Statesman* for *The Times Literary Supplement*, held at his flat in Beaufort Street. The atmosphere there was rather different.

At the Group, alcohol on the premises was banned, though anyone with a thirst could slip out to the pub in the interval which came half way through the proceedings. By outsiders, this rule of ours was much mocked, and when the Group began to attract publicity, we would find ourselves characterised as a band of severely puritan teetotalers.

Arriving at George Fraser's flat, one discovered that an immense bottle party was in progress. The room was filled with smoke and noise, and new arrivals were constantly pushing their way in. While his wife Paddy opened the door and welcomed new-comers, George would try to maintain some kind of order, asking those who had brought manuscripts to read them in turn. After the reading he would ask for comments. If these came from the Scottish poet Burns Singer, who functioned as a kind of resident gadfly, uproar would break out, which the host vainly attempted to still by passing round further supplies of beer and wine.

If Singer's fierce tongue was a disruptive factor, so too was the attitude of Group members. Though we were nearly all of us poor and struggling, we felt no attraction towards the old Bohemia of the forties, which we identified with some of the other poets present. Our usual way of baiting the company was for one or other of us to read a poem by Ted Hughes. A favourite was 'The Martyrdom of Bishop Farrar', later to be the final item in Ted's first book, *The Hawk in the Rain*:

> *The sullen-jowled watching Welsh townspeople*
> *Hear him crack in the fire's mouth; they see what*
> *Black oozing twist of stuff bubbles the smell*
> *That tars and retches their lungs: no pulpit*
> *Of his ever held their eyes so still,*
> *Never, as now his agony, his wit.*

Perhaps because his talent was on the very threshold of an acceptance which would alter the existing poetic geography, opposition to what Hughes did was, at this moment, and in this circle, especially fierce.

But there were lighter moments than this at George's gatherings. Who could forget, for example the Anglo-Indian poet who read an interminable poem about Simla in a mournful and barely audible voice? The poem showed an obsession with exact topography – the two lines I remember ran:

The streets run up and down,
And the streets run across and across

When the poem ended, a total, and for the place and circumstances, totally exceptional, silence fell. George, whose kindness and good nature were and are legendary, pulled himself together and uttered a few rather subdued compliments. Instead of being placated by these, the indignant poet burst out with: 'You say that, George. Yet you never print my poems in the *Times Literary Supplement*. Why don't you print this one, George?' Whereupon another and even deeper silence fell.

Our collective appearances at George's bottle-parties were, perhaps, the thing which first began to get the Group talked about. We were soon to realize that the rest of the literary world viewed us in no very favourable light. There are certain conventions which a young poet flouts at his peril – and one of these is the convention of individuality. The Movement poets had obeyed it by resisting the Movement label; by saying, frequently, that they felt they had little in common with one another. The members of the Group, on the other hand, could not deny their own inter-connection. Indeed, it must have seemed, from outside, that we seemed to boast of it. We made things worse because we were not modest. The articulacy we had developed in private soon became a weapon which we employed in public.

Meanwhile, some of the more prominent members of the Group were publishing their first collections of poetry; and the literary situation itself was changing round us. Peter Redgrove's *The Collector* appeared early in 1960; Peter Porter's *Once Bitten, Twice Bitten* and my own *A Tropical Childhood* came out in 1961. Had these books been published a little earlier, they would have seemed – at least in the case of Porter and Redgrove – a direct and calculated riposte to the Movement poets. But already things were becoming more complicated.

The cult of Lowell's poetry which sprang up in England in the early 1960's was, primarily, an expression of English feelings about what was happening to natively English literature. The most powerful expression of these feelings is to be found in the preface which A. Alvarez wrote for his Penguin anthology *The New Poetry*, published in 1962, and soon to become the bible of a new generation of poetry-readers. In this preface, Alvarez launched an attack on what he called 'the gentility principle'. 'My own feeling,' he concluded, 'is that a good deal of poetic talent exists in England at the moment. But whether or not it will come to anything depends not on the machinations of any literary racket but on the degree to which the poets can remain immune to the disease so often found in English culture: gentility.' . . .

The chief consequence of Alvarez's anthology was a surge of enthusiasm for so-called 'confessional verse'. Confessional verse was stringently defined. It had to be of American origin. English writers with distinctly 'confessional' tendencies – they range from Martin Bell to Elizabeth Jennings – were either ignored, or else dismissed as 'embarrassing'. What fascinated English critics, all of a sudden, was Freudian rhetoric, the monologue from the analyst's couch. Yet they never seemed to recognise how much the technique had been honed by encounters with psychiatry; they never remarked on the mask – that of the patient undergoing analysis – which the American poet often wore over his more usual and everyday face. It was as if, in paying homage to forthright personal poetry of this type, the English were, at the same time, making a masochistic acknowledgement of the superiority of American literature. Just as Britain was, in the world of international politics, inexorably losing the importance she had once possessed; so too, it began to be assumed that American poetry was automatically superior to anything being written in England.

As they emerged into a more public arena, with the publication of *A Group Anthology* in 1963, the Group poets bore the brunt of this assumption, just as they suffered by comparison with Hughes's glamour. The collection did not receive nearly such a good press as Conquest's *New Lines*, which had preceded it by eight years, though it is worth noting that a number of the contributors were soon tacitly accepted as writers who deserved attention.

Yet I must now admit that the publication of the anthology marks, in my own mind, the point at which the Group started to decline. The hostility aroused by the book – on the one hand by those who felt it threatened an established orthodoxy, and on the other by those who thought it was not adventurous enough – was a minor matter. And the furious protests of those who scented a cabal would soon die down. What did the damage was success. The publicity generated by the book brought in more and more recruits. Meetings in my two small rooms in Sydney Street were packed to suffocation, Friday after Friday. In such circumstances, the quality of the discussions could only go down. It fell, first, because there were now too many people present for the early intimacy to be maintained; and second, because there were too many aspiring poets who wanted to read, which meant that we lost our old sense of continuity.

But there was another problem as well, less to do with the Group in particular than with the position of the poet in England. Thanks to the Penguin Modern Poets series (financed by the money earned from the paperback edition of *Lady Chatterley*) contemporary poetry reached a wider and wider audience in England during the sixties. This tempted poets to think of themselves as professionals, in the sense that there were already professional painters and professional musicians. We, in the Group, were not exempt from this feeling. And we were growing older. Faced with the problem, not only of self-definition, but of what we were to do for a living, we chose different solutions. Some of us, as I have said, worked for a while in advertising, but never with any great faith in this as a permanent way of life. Some went to the universities (in spite of everything); one to an art-school; MacBeth continued his career in the BBC. More crucial than the precise source of income was the vision which each poet had of himself. Some saw poetry as a primary activity, which another occupation must sustain. A few, with the upsurge of Pop poetry, saw the poet's role as being to occupy the Tom Tiddler's ground between the guru and the entertainer. My own reactions were different. I could not accept either of these as the solution.

As the years went by, as the Group continued to meet under my chairmanship, I was faced with a number of problems. One was to do with judgement, and I can locate it in a quotation from Northrop Frye. 'The sense of value,' he says, 'is an individual, unpredictable, variable, incommunicable, indemonstrable, and mainly intuitive reaction to knowledge. In knowledge, the context of the work of literature is literature; in value-judgement, the context of the work of literature is the reader's experience.' My judgement was now being increasingly influenced by experience of modern art, through my practice as a critic. This opened a gap in communication with most of those who came to my house on Friday evenings.

More important, there was my own view of myself and what I was doing, now changing to something which I thought the other members of the Group might not find sympathetic. I did not want to be a professional poet, though I did want to be a professional writer – an ambition I had now gone some distance towards achieving, and which I was eventually to fulfil. Poetry was becoming for me, not so much a process of making, or of communication, but a deliberate act of self-discovery. The poem, by insisting on finding its own shape, its own imagery, its own system of inclusions and omissions, could often reveal to me that what I did feel was in fact different from what I thought I felt.

I came to think of my poetry as being like a stream which flowed through the kind of limestone country I had known as a child in Jamaica. At times it flowed murmuring and hidden, in a way that only I was aware of, a faint whisper in some remote hollow of the brain. At other times it burst upwards, and could be seen rushing along in the light, deep or shallow according to the lie of the land. I hoped that, like those Jamaican streams, it ran direct and clear, but for the time at least I began to find arguments about technique irrelevant. And arguments about content were positively unhelpful, because more and more I wanted this to choose itself, unprompted by my own or any other consciousness, as an expression of the dialogue I heard at all times going on within me.

Though I was now a skilful chairman, I felt dishonest when I exercised these skills every Friday evening, while hugging to myself the knowledge of my own reservations, and of the fact that my submission to the democracy Philip had insisted on from the start was only external. In the circumstances, and after ten good years, it seemed to me time to call a halt.

The Burnt Child, Gollancz